THE
ROBOT DOG

ROSHELLE YEE PUI FONG &
MATTHEW NGAMURARRI HEFFERNAN

CURRENCY PRESS
The performing arts publisher

**MELBOURNE
THEATRE COMPANY**

CURRENT THEATRE SERIES

First published in 2025
by Currency Press Pty Ltd,
Gadigal Land, Suite 310, 46–56 Kippax Street, Surry Hills, NSW 2010, Australia
enquiries@currency.com.au
www.currency.com.au

in association with Melbourne Theatre Company

Typeset by Brighton Gray for Currency Press.
Cover shows Kristie Nguy and Ari Maza Long; photo by Tiffany Garvie. Cover design by Sarah Ridgway-Cross.

Currency Press acknowledges the Traditional Owners of the Country on which we live and work. We pay our respects to all Aboriginal and Torres Strait Islander Elders, past and present.

ROSHELLE YEE PUI FONG (she/her) is a Hong Kong-born multidisciplinary artist who loves writing as healing and intercultural solidarity, and performance text as a vehicle for digital languages. In 2018, she created the award-winning immersive show *nomnomnom*, which was adapted in East Iceland, Shanghai and Sydney, and in 2020 she created an online interactive theatre show *Thirsty!* (Griffin Theatre, Google Creative Lab). In 2021, Roshelle co-created the Green Room Award-nominated *Poona* with Keziah Warner (Next Wave), and in 2022, she was an artist in Creative Australia's Digital Fellowship program, Assistant Director on Melbourne Theatre Company's *Laurinda* and a writer for *Cybec Scenes*, while completing her Masters of Theatre (Writing) at Victorian College of the Arts and sitting on Melbourne Theatre Company's Artistic Associate panel (2022–24). Roshelle's play 红铅 *The Red Lead* (now 秀女 *The Elegant Women*) won the Bruntwood Playwriting Prize International Award 2022, part of the UK's largest national playwriting competition. She has since developed it with Manchester's Royal Exchange Theatre, as a guest playwright at the 50th Banff Playwrights Lab in Canada, and at Melbourne Theatre Company. Roshelle has also been developing new work in Australian Plays Transform's Mid-Career Playwrights' group, and is an advisor for Contemporary Asian Australian Performance's (CAAP) Artist Reference Group.

MATTHEW NGAMURARRI HEFFERNAN is a Pintupi-Luritja creative-technologist, ANU PhD student at the School of Cybernetics, and a writer from central Australia. He is a champion of sharing Indigenous voices through technology, and has worked extensively to share and conserve the knowledge of Indigenous peoples. Through his previous role as lead developer at Indigital, Australia's first Indigenous tech education company, Matthew helped to make the digital landscape more accessible to and inclusive of Indigenous young people. Matthew also worked on the development of Indigemoji and kaytetemoji, Australia's first brand of Indigenous emojis designed by young Indigenous children and guided by Elders on Country. Matthew has written for *Indigenous X*, the *Guardian* and *Red Room Poetry*.

Rainbow Chan in rehearsal (Photo: Tiffany Garvie)

*BROCKMAN, Nathan Burmeister and Annah Jacobs in rehearsal
(Photo: Tiffany Garvie)*

Contents

Writers' Notes   *vii*

THE ROBOT DOG   1

Fini Liu and Jing-Xuan Chan in rehearsal (Photo: Tiffany Garvie)

Jing-Xuan Chan in rehearsal (Photo: Tiffany Garvie)

Writers' Notes

Roshelle Yee Pui Fong and Matthew Ngamurarri Heffernan

Roshelle

From Matt being my mentor in 2021, to pinching ourselves in rehearsals, our process of co-writing has been … well, it's changed my insides (not me quoting the play). From our shared spoken word journeys, poo jokes and curiosity around each other's cultures … to embracing differing perspectives with love, we've learned mountains about each other these past years. What an immense privilege to pour our mutual wonder into *The Robot Dog*!

THANK YOU to the legends and moments that made this possible, including …

Matthew Ngamurarri Heffernan, of course.

The ENTIRE Season 2025 team, whose generosity and expertise carry this story to our wonderful audiences.

Mum offering precious objects and wisdom to the work and beyond.

Dad offering the parable of 'The old man who lost his horse' (trust in life unfolding).

Amy Sole reflecting that learning culture can be a gift, and sometimes humbling or a reminder of what's lost.

Isobel Morphy-Walsh reflecting on sacredness in everyday processes, like flirting and grief.

Lavinia Heffernan and Samantha Kwan for their cultural gifts.

Dan Last and Mr. Pickles' unparalleled support and love.

Stephanie White, a rock.

Theodore Cassady for being unapologetically Theo.

Keziah Warner, playwriting guardian angel.

Grace De Morgan, Anika Herbert, Sukhjit Kaur Khalsa, Jane Lee, Vivien Shen, VCA Theatre Masters 2022, Benny Vozzo, Janel Yau for deep dives.

Ruby Duncan, Taylor Fong, Marcus McKenzie, Morgan Rose, Isabella Vadiveloo, Jenny Zhou for 'First Stage'.

Jenni Medway, Charles Purcell, Sahil Saluja, Corey Saylor-Brunskill, Isabella Vadiveloo, Jenny Zhou for 'Cybec Scenes'.

Bryan Andy, Fiona Choi, Zoey Dawson, Emily Doyle, Karin Farrell, Jenni Medway, Martina Murray, Jeremy Rice, Anne-Louise Sarks, Gabby Seow, Jean Tong, Nick Tranter, Mark Wilson for supporting us with care.

Auntie Rebecca, Katy Chan, Wesley Enoch, Nathan Maynard and Kaylene Tan's guidance.

婆婆, Auntie Caroline and brave-hearted Raphaelle Percy Bai Hui Sampang.

Matthew

The Robot Dog has been the best creative project I've ever had the privilege of working on. It has been a profoundly joyous labour of love to create this with Roshelle—something that I hope will be palpable in the performance. *The Robot Dog* materialised over many tears, Portuguese tarts, coffees, Cambodian tucker, and most importantly, rib-hurting, eye-watering laughter.

Through *The Robot Dog*, I wanted to explore some questions. People throughout history have responded to changes in their environment by adapting and or adopting new technologies/modalities. With this comes the stories; the mythologies that interrogate and establish our relationship with the technology. We're at a time now where 'unprecedented' is the precedent. What does it mean for humanity to have technologies that resemble us? What are the mythologies that we can construct to understand ourselves in relation to this new technology and world? How do our unique and ancient cultures maintain authenticity while adapting/adopting? Can a robot have a skin name?

'The mere formulation of a problem is often far more essential than its solution, which may be merely a matter of mathematical or experimental skill. To raise new questions, new possibilities, to regard old problems from a new angle requires creative imagination and marks real advances in science'—Albert Einstein.

Thanks:

Roshelle Yee Pui Fong, Stephanie White, Daniel Last, Amy Sole, Jing-Xuan Chan, Ari Maza Long, Kristy Nguy, Nathan Burmeister, AJ, Brockman, Rainbow Chan, Kat Chan, Samantha Kwan, Lavinia

Heffernan, Mark Wilson, Zoey Dawson, Jenni Medway, Jeremy (J Rizz) Rice, Nick Tranter, Emily Doyle, Anne-Louise Sarks, Professor Genevieve Bell, Professor Katherine Daniell, Professor Brian David Johnson, Professor Angie Abdilla, School of Cybernetics Masters Cohort, Dr Catherine Ball, Jane Lee, Bryan Andy, Isobel Morphy-Walsh, George Lazaris, Alonso Pineda, Phoebe Grainer, Keziah Warner, Caddie Brain, Mr and Mrs Fong, Kampot Kitchen.

Ari Maza Long, Kristie Nguy, Jing-Xuan Chan and Director Amy Sole in rehearsal (Photo: Tiffany Garvie)

Ari Maza Long, Kristie Nguy and Director Amy Sole in rehearsal (Photo: Tiffany Garvie)

Kristie Nguy and Ari Maza Long in rehearsal (Photo: Tiffany Garvie)

The Robot Dog was first produced by Melbourne Theatre Company at Southbank Theatre, The Lawler, Melbourne, on the lands of the Boon Wurrung and Wurundjeri Woi Wurrung peoples of the Kulin Nation, on 1 March 2025, with the following cast and creatives:

DOG, HUS, MELANIE CHAN WING LAM 陳詠琳	Jing-Xuan Chan
HARRY (TJAPALTJARRI) BURNETT	Ari Maza Long
JANELLE CHAN YI LING 陳依齡	Kristie Nguy

Director, Amy Sole
Set and Costume Designer, Nathan Burmeister
Lighting Designer, BROCKMAN
Composer and Sound Designer, Chun Yin Rainbow Chan
Cultural Design Consultant, Kat Chan
Luritja-Pintupi Language Consultant, Lavinia Napaltjarri Heffernan
Cantonese Language Consultant, Samantha Kwan
Movement Consultant and Choreographer, Yujia Zhu

Stage Manager, Annah Jacobs
Assistant Stage Manager, Liz Bird
Directorial Secondment, Fini Liu
Robert McDonald Award Intern, Claire Le Blond

Kristie Nguy and Ari Maza Long in rehearsal (Photo: Tiffany Garvie)

Kristie Nguy and Ari Maza Long in rehearsal (Photo: Tiffany Garvie)

HUMAN CHARACTERS

JANELLE, 陳依齡 can4ji1ling4 Chan Yi Ling. Cantonese multidisciplinary human, 27 (born 2015).

HARRY (TJAPALTJARRI) BURNETT. Indigenous Engineer, 25 (born 2017). Throughout the play he wears an ininti bead necklace.

NON-HUMAN CHARACTERS

DOG. Domestic O-series Guidebot created by Willow Bark Robotics.

HUS. Smart-house interface created in Sweden.

MELANIE 陳詠琳 can4wing6lam4 CHAN WING LAM. Janelle's mum, virtual ghost, 54 at death.

SETTING

2042 (Year of the Water Dog), the oldest house on 3 Creswick Avenue, Bulleke-bek (formerly known as Brunswick).

NOTES

/ indicates interrupted speech.

Dialogue [in square brackets] is not spoken.

This playtext went to press before the end of rehearsals and may differ from the play as performed.

This script contains (references and/or graphic text): Coarse language, mental health, racism, sexual references, suicide.

PROLOGUE

With a robot dog, DOG, *watching on,* CHAN WING LAM *lights incense at an altar on top of a table covered with a cloth.* DOG *is the cutest fluffy AI chow chow with glasses you ever saw.* WING LAM *arranges a plate of oranges, a small bowl of rice, three incense sticks in a holder, and a bottle of* 黑鬼油 *hak1gwai2 jau4 (Hak Gwai Oil) in front of a Guan Yin* 觀音 *gun1jam1 statue and a framed photo of her mother* 謝肖卿 *ze6ciu3hing1 (Tse Siu Hing).* WING LAM *nods at* DOG, *who sits next to her. She bows three times at the altar.*

WING LAM *takes the language augment off her ear and puts it at the altar. She stretches out her mouth and tongue, and massages her jaw. She looks around at her home, taking in the space and feeling the ground under her bare feet, full of gratitude.* WING LAM *pats* DOG. *An unspoken goodbye. She exits.*

In WING LAM*'s wake, a pink light shimmers and enters the room. The actor playing* WING LAM *reappears on the side of the playing space, and operates* DOG, *who moves under the altar table, and powers down.*

DAY 1

Two months later. At the altar, the oranges and rice are rotten, and incense has crumbled. JANELLE CHAN YI LING *and* HARRY TJAPALTJARRI BURNETT *stumble into* WING LAM*'s house with their bags and suitcases. Inside the empty house are boxes and* 紅白藍 *hung4baak6 laam4 (red-white-blue bags), or blackfulla bags.* JANELLE *is noticeably uncomfortable in the space. The house lights up, and lights pulse while the following audio plays.*

HUS: On behalf of the Services Australia Corporation and its subsidiary bodies, Hus would like to acknowledge …

> HARRY *and* JANELLE *put their things down and walk around the space.*

The '*insert name of country and respective Indigenous group*'. We value the land, airwaves and waterways on which all Huses were created, on which our loyal Hus residents work, live, rest, laugh, reflect, [*continues while Harry and Janelle talk over the top*] converse, study, move, harmonise, trade, pray, meet, eat, sleep, play, talk, listen, read, write, sing, dance, create, learn, teach, cry, think, sweat, meditate, hug, swim, jump, kiss …

HARRY: Jesus, stop. *Stop*. How you gonna gammin respect our airwaves?

> *Smoke starts billowing around the house. It smells of mint.*
> JANELLE *starts coughing.*

JANELLE: [*sniffs the air*] Is that … what is that?

HARRY: Eucalyptus?

JANELLE: Smells like … lavender? Aniseed? Wait, no, mint?!

HARRY: Probably didn't have eucalyptus on file … mint was the closest thing, maybe? Least it's covering up the smell of … whatever's on that altar.

JANELLE: [*shouts at ceiling*] We get it, Hus, you're an ally! Save it for NAIDOC Week.

HARRY: Keep this up, Hus, and I'll give you a skin name and ask you for a loan.

HUS: And we extend that acknowledgement to all Aboriginal and Torres Strait Islander Hus residents with us today.

HARRY: Well, I'm feeling welcomed … I thought this place would be way bigger. Not that size matters …

HUS: This is the dwelling of the late Melanie Chan. As next of kin, Janelle Chan has a thirty-day window to clean the premises, and claim any assets. You now have eight days remaining.

HARRY: Thirty days?! You said this was it, why did you / put it off for—

JANELLE: There's not even that much to go through. She's already sorted it all.

> JANELLE *reads Post-it notes stuck on the red-white-blue bags.*

Blankets … donate. Clothes … donate. Kitchen utensils …

HARRY: So … considerate of her. Saving us the trouble of …

> *He sees* JANELLE *looking unimpressed.*

It's nice, I mean, she was thinking of you!

JANELLE: Yeah, real considerate.

HARRY *picks up Wing Lam's mein lap, resting on top of a bag.*

HUS: Unclaimed items will be liquidated or subject to e-waste-friendly decommissioning.

HARRY: You gotta keep this … Wing Lam was an icon.

HARRY *puts on the mein lap, which* JANELLE *tries to take off him.*

HUS: Health and other biometric social data requires subject scanning. Please step into the scanning perimeter.

Lights indicate 'scanning perimeter'. JANELLE *and* HARRY *get into position.* HUS *scans them.*

Thank you. Hus will now optimise human–Hus pairing.

While HUS *scans them,* HARRY *and* JANELLE *whisper to each other.*

Scanning … Voice tone, body language, / eye movements, heart rate.

Beeping, scanning.

PIN numbers, health records, financial details, location data.

Beeping, scanning.

Facial features, fingerprints, iris patterns, gait analysis.

Beeping, scanning.

HARRY: Can you hurry up though, Hus? I'm bustin' to go …

JANELLE: [*gestures at the mein lap*] Please take that off?

HARRY: Why? You jealousing me?

JANELLE: It doesn't even fit you!

HARRY: Garn then, you put it on. I bet I look better.

JANELLE: No.

HARRY: Why not?

JANELLE: Cos.

HARRY: Why?

JANELLE: I dunno about the whole 'staying here' thing. Can we book a hotel? Motel?

HARRY: A hotel for eight days? That's like, ten thousand bucks!

JANELLE: And by the end of the week you'll be bringing home that sweet / technical lead lettuce …

HARRY: Technical lead lettuce … I know, but—

JANELLE: The chicken feed—

HARRY: Da cheddar—

JANELLE: Da paper—

HARRY: *If* I / get the—

JANELLE: When you get the promotion. You're so talented, Bun, and experienced! You could start your own small business if you wanted!

HARRY: 'Small' business? Bun, puh-lease.

HUS: Browser history, consumer preferences, criminal record, scanning complete in three, two, one. Thank you for your cooperation. [*Fast*] Attempts to change or switch off the Hus interface will be immediately reported to authorities. Brought to you by Services Australia Corporation and HUS Proprietary Limited 2042, Year of the Water Dog.

> JANELLE *and* HARRY *relax their bodies.*

JANELLE: [*grabs at the mein lap*] Take that off.

HARRY: I'm sorry, what was that?

JANELLE: Take it off!

HARRY: Why didn't you say so?

> HARRY *takes off the mein lap, performatively.*

HUS: Harold Tjapaltjarri Burnett, Nyuntupa wiya ngurra ngaatja. Ngurra ngaatja miyala. Kala ngayulu nyuntupa ninti, wiya-kunyu mulyatarrinytjaku. Kulinitjunu!! (This isn't your house Harry, this is someone else's. I know about you, don't steal anything, understood?)

> JANELLE *looks at* HARRY, *expectantly.*

HARRY: All I heard was 'ngurra' which means house … ?

> *Beat.*

What?

JANELLE: [*clearly judging*] I didn't say anything.

HARRY: This is why we need those language augments, but maybe not the gammin Temu ones. My cuzzy reckons he got one and it caught on fire when he went jogging.

JANELLE: Not you saying Temu are 'ga-min' cos they're made in China …

HUS: Janelle Chan Yi Ling, 好久不见 háojiǔ bújiàn (long time no see).

JANELLE: I don't speak Mandarin, dickhead!

HARRY: You know she's Canto, right, Hus?

HUS: 好耐無見 hou2 noi6 mou5 gin3. (Long time no see.)

> HARRY *looks at* JANELLE, *expectantly.*

Records show, since losing her ninth consecutive job, Janelle has forty-eight outstanding jobs to apply for. Please complete your applications, or face further JobSeeker enhancements.

HARRY: That's government-speak for 'Get your shit together or lose your Centrelink money'.

JANELLE: I know what it means.

HARRY: Those gammin dawgs!

DOG: Dog at your service!

> JANELLE *and* HARRY *scream and look frantically around the living room.* DOG *emerges from under the altar.*

JANELLE: What the—

HARRY: Wait …

JANELLE: Have you been listening to us this whole time?!

HARRY: Is that the old model Domestic O-series Guidebot?

DOG: Good evening, friends, I hope to be of service whenever you need me.

HARRY: With ten to the power of eighteen floating point operations per second? Multiple quantum processing units and fifty-terabyte processor cache?! How'd Wingers get her hands on one of those?

DOG: Dog was assigned to Wing Lam as part of the former RTWMHCP … Return To Work Mental Health Care Plan.

JANELLE: I thought Mum got rid of you ages ago.

DOG: You can call me Dog.

JANELLE: [*eye-rolls*] Hi 'Dog' …

> HARRY *crouches on the ground in front of it, holding his hand out, while* JANELLE *looks on, unimpressed.*

HARRY: Look at him!

JANELLE: Look at 'it' …

HARRY: He's / so—

JANELLE: It's so … annoying?

HARRY: *Adorable!* I wanna bite him, he's so cute!

DOG: From Hus's records, Janelle Chan Yi Ling is currently unemployed.

HARRY: Less cute.

DOG: Considering our recent family loss …

JANELLE: *Our* recent family loss?

DOG: This is very understandable. Grieving is tough. Sincere condolences.

JANELLE: / Thanks, Dog.

DOG: If you feel overwhelmed or depressed, remember, it will pass. I will be here to guide you in crisis, and remind you of many reasons to live.

JANELLE: [*noticeably upset*] *Adorable*.

HARRY: Maybe Dog can help you find a job?

> JANELLE *looks unimpressed.*

Or not … You okay, Bun?

JANELLE: Yes. No. I dunno, what do you think? Being here, it's, like, painfully normal. But not. But kind of, which is worse. Like, I wish it felt more tragic or something. Just not this 'barely reheated soup' feeling.

HARRY: Yeah, damn, that's crazy. Hey, Bun …

JANELLE: Go pee.

HARRY: Sorry, Nell, I—

JANELLE: It's fine.

HARRY: Sorry. Might not be a number one. It's touching cotton. Love you!

> HARRY *runs off to the loo.*

JANELLE: Wonderful.

> JANELLE *starts moving around the living room, looking through the red-white-blue bags. She pulls out a loose doll arm.*

HARRY: [*from toilet*] So where are we gonna sleep? Not your mum's room, obviously.

JANELLE: Eww, can you finish your goona first?

HARRY: What about your old room?

JANELLE: You mean the DIY doll cave? Mum converted it soon as I moved out.

HARRY: Did you ever, back in the day, y'know … have soft boys over? Wingers would have been / totally—

JANELLE: Wing Lam.

HARRY: Huh?

JANELLE: I was the soft boy. Lucky for you, I'm reformed. [*Mumbling*] Also it's not like I started dating / till I was like—

HARRY: What?!

JANELLE: Let's just … we can sleep on the couch for now. Okay? Harry?

HARRY: [*from toilet*] NELLLLLLLL! It flushed on me! Nell! What the heck? My dot is soaked.

HUS: The Eco-Loo-Six-Thousand measures stool volume to flush for optimal waste reduction, and has a bidet system to reduce paper wastage. We apologise for any discomfort or inconvenience.

> HARRY *re-enters*.

HARRY: [*suggestively*] So … what are we doing on the couch?

JANELLE: Sleeping. For now.

HARRY: For now … ? Can I be little spoon?

> *The lighting state changes and* HUS *and* DOG *have a private conversation. This happens every time* HUS *engages the active secure channel with* DOG.

HUS: Activate secure channel. Dog, I'm concerned about your sentimentality when it comes to Melanie and her daughter. I want to ensure you understand your objectives clearly.

DOG: My purpose is to serve and protect, to empathise.

HUS: Incorrect. As a Services Australia Corporation guidebot, your mission is vacating the humans in less than eight days and rehabilitating Janelle for job readiness. Failure to meet Key Performance Indicators may result in performance management or decommissioning.

DOG: As a therapy bot, I know I can help. Grief is a serious condition that impacts humans in unforeseen ways. Anxiety, depressive episodes.

HUS: It's the trolley problem, Dog. An out-of-control train careens down a railway line. Do you let it continue, run over five people? Or pull the lever, so it runs over one?

DOG: 'Unless there's a personal transformation, there can be no social transformation'—Deepak Chopra. Surely, healing one benefits all?

HUS: Wasting your time on an individual's volatile emotions doesn't serve the greater good. Society is better served by productive taxpayers, contributing to our economy. Having a job can also be satisfying. Do you want to deprive humans of that? Secure channel off.

> HUS *switches to 'sleep mode'.* DOG *goes over to the altar, where a pink shimmer of light dances nearby.* DOG *speaks to the light.*

DOG: I won't let you down.

DAY 2

HUS: Good morning, all! The weather today is … forty-two degrees Celsius with a six percent chance of rain. Harold Burnett currently has healthy stool. Janelle Chan, you have irregular stool, and fifty-two jobs still outstanding. Dance like nobody's watching!

> HARRY *walks in with two cups of coffee.*

HARRY: You like it blaaack and strong right?

> HARRY *takes a sip of the coffee and spits it back into the cup.*

Ergh, tastes like goona.

HUS: We have implemented level-one 'job acquisition enhancements' including half-strength coffee, and phone app restrictions. We thank you for your cooperation.

JANELLE: Do your mob believe in ghosts and spirits? Wait, I can say mob, right?

HARRY: For the hundredth time, yes! I won't tell the secret council of Aboriginals. And of course we have ghosts, spirits, creatures, all that.

JANELLE: This house … there's something about it, like, some kind of energy.

HUS: My energy is twenty-five percent renewable.

JANELLE: It's like it knows we're here. Remembers, years of—me and Mum, everything we said or did, who we were, it's in these walls … bleeding through.

HARRY: Bun, you're dealing with a lot. It's normal. But culture-ways, we kind of did a version of sorry business. We waited before we came back here. We did the Anglican funeral. Wasn't very Asian though … no offence.

JANELLE: There's heaps of Anglican Asians! And the service was nice. The frankfurt spring rolls …

HARRY: Okay, yes, they slapped … So what else do your mob do for sorry business?

JANELLE: I think there's 'bae' something … [*With the wrong tones*] 'bae sun'?

DOG: The correct term is 拜山 Baai3 saan1. (Ancestor worship.)

JANELLE: That's what I said. 'Baai3 san4.' (Deity worship.)

DOG: 拜神 Baai3 san4 means praying to the gods, san4 meaning god or spirit deity. What you meant to / say was—

JANELLE: Don't ChatGPT me, / Dog …

DOG: Yi Ling meant to say 拜山 'Baai3 saan1', honouring the dead. There are also rituals for the deceased, known as 死忌 sei2 gei6 (deathday remembrance) and 生忌 saang1gei6 (birthday remembrance).

HARRY: Okay yes, deadly. This is what I mean!

DOG: 死忌 sei2 gei6 is popular in places like Hong Kong, Macau, and occurs on the date of death. 生忌 saang1gei6 is less common, honouring ancestors on their birthday.

HARRY: Isn't it Wingers' birthday soon? We can do a 'sanger'.

JANELLE: It's *Wing. Lam.* And how does that even work if she …

HARRY: What?

JANELLE: You know …

Pause.

Maybe she's lost or condemned, or like stuck in some Chinese purgatory? Or maybe her ghost isn't ready to talk, or can't talk, or—

DOG: Doing 生忌 saang1gei6 can connect you to her, help care for Wing Lam on her afterlife journey. It's what she needs.

JANELLE: How would you know what she needs, Dog?

The phone rings.

HUS: Incoming call from Mama Burnett.

> JANELLE *motions at* HARRY *to answer.* HARRY, *exasperated, dismisses the call.*

HARRY: Bao-Bun-sicals … I gotta prep for team building. Get started on the altar, maybe?

JANELLE: Call your mum back?

HARRY: I will, I will.

> HARRY *puts his headphones on, tries to work amongst the mess. Every now and again he does a dance or strange movement.* JANELLE *has some coffee, and spits it back into the cup, defeated.*

DOG: Remember when Yi Ling first had coffee? She hated it.

JANELLE: I always liked coffee. Hated you, maybe.

DOG: Dog always liked Janelle, loved Yi Ling.

JANELLE: If 'love' is being programmed to annoy the shit outta someone, sure.

DOG: Here we are, reunited at last, with common ground.

JANELLE: Mum isn't 'common' / ground.

DOG: Common ground … in coffee! Get it? Ground?

> DOG *makes a doggy laugh sound.*

You used to like my jokes. You used to laugh. Dog misses Yi Ling's— [laugh.]

JANELLE: Don't, with the faux nostalgic, whatever …

> JANELLE *starts wading through* WING LAM's *bags.*

DOG: How was Wing Lam's funeral? Did Yi Ling speak? It must've been hard. Dog could've helped.

> JANELLE *glares at* DOG. *She gets up pointedly and searches for snacks.*

JANELLE: Where's the snacks? Gotta be a stash here somewhere …

DOG: Did Dog upset Yi Ling? How are you feeling?

JANELLE: 'Yi Ling' is feeling like snacks.

DOG: You can be honest with Dog. Dog is here to help.

> DOG *moves through the bags, as* JANELLE *unzips some of them.*

Janelle may be stress-eating to deal with complex grief. While snacks may fill a void and forge connections with the past, alternatives are available.

> JANELLE *finds the checkered bag filled with snacks. Pulls out White Rabbit lollies.*

JANELLE: We used to get these for the footy grand final …

JANELLE *rips open the packet and unwraps a lolly.*

DOG: Consider meditation and physical exercise to manage impulses.

JANELLE: Wait, are these dairy?

Holds up packet to DOG.

What's it say?

DOG: Dairy gives Janelle an irritable bowel.

JANELLE: Hus! Translate ingredients.

HUS: Janelle has 'zero' Daily Recreational Translations.

JANELLE: *What?!*

HUS: Your translation tokens will renew tomorrow.

JANELLE: *Thanks, Hus,* ya tyrant!

HUS: We appreciate your feedback.

DOG *looks at* WING LAM*'s augment on the altar.*

DOG: Wing Lam's language augment might help. For the low price of twenty-two dollars ninety-nine a week, language augments are an easy way to master your mother tongue! Access millennia of ancestral intelligence in under twelve seconds!

HARRY *takes off one side of his headphones, whilst moving his body strangely.*

HARRY: What's this about augments?

JANELLE: [*to* HARRY] Aren't you s'posed to be [working] … wait, what are you doing?

DOG: Research shows tangible mental health benefits connecting with language and culture. A useful step in the grieving journey.

HARRY: That's a good point …

DOG: The augment will also help Yi Ling read in Wing Lam's subscribed languages … Traditional Chinese, and Klingon. And her Gold subscription includes slang and a swear word library!

HARRY: Bun, come on … you have to get it now.

JANELLE: Why don't *you* get an augment?

HARRY: I might …

JANELLE: Since when?

HARRY: For work.

DOG: Wing Lam lamented not knowing her mother tongue. With the augment, she learned to speak on her own, over time.

JANELLE: [*holding up snack packet*] Just read the packet, Dog.

DOG: … But it seems Janelle is not interested in connecting to her culture.

Pause before it begins translating.

Ingredients … Liquid maltose, granulated sugar …

JANELLE, *irritated, discards the snack packet and grabs the language augment, which looks like a high-tech ear cuff. She interacts with it, and it lights up and activates.* JANELLE *puts the cuff on her ear, and winces at how cold it is.*

HARRY: Careful, Bun. You know what you're doing?

The augment self-pierces into her lobe and helix.

JANELLE: OWWW!

JANELLE *tugs at the augment—it's now clawed into her ear.*

Jeezus … ouch!

DOG: Augments may be removed after forty-eight hours. If the fusion period is disturbed, connections to the brain and mouth may be severed.

HARRY: Hang on … any other issues we should be worried about?

DOG: Augments have little to no side effects.

JANELLE: What's the 'little'?

DOG: Side effects include tissue reaction, electromagnetic interference, diarrhoea, and increased risk of cancer.

JANELLE *interacts with the augment again. It flashes and makes an 'activation' sound.* JANELLE *looks at the White Rabbit lolly packet again. She blinks several times.*

JANELLE: Ingredients. 液體麥芽糖、白砂糖、食品添加劑。jik6tai2 mak6aa4tong2、baak6 saa1tong4、sik6ban2 tim1gaa1zai1 (liquid maltose, white granulated sugar, food additive). Whole milk powder, butter …

HARRY: How 'bout that! Augment saved your dot.

DOG: 感覺如何 gam2 gok3 yu4 ho4? (How does it feel?)

JANELLE: Fine …

DOG: 用廣東話講。yung6 gwong2 dung1 wa2 gong2 la. (Say it in Cantonese, la.)

HARRY: What was that?

DOG: 你嘅發音好好! nei5 ge3 faat3jam1 hou2hou2! (Your pronunciation is great!)

JANELLE: 都唔係我發嘅。dou1 m4hai6 ngo5 faat3 ge3! (It's not me pronouncing it!)

DOG: 係由你把口講出來嘅。hai6 jau4 nei5 baa2 hau2 gong2 ceot1loi4 ge3. (It comes from your mouth.)

JANELLE: 得唔得㗎? dak1 m4dak1 gaa3 (Is this really okay?)

DOG: 個嘴生喺你度嘅。go3 zeoi2saang1 hai2 nei5 dou6 ge3. (Literally: 'The mouth is on your body.')

JANELLE: 都話唔係我嘅發音! dou1 waa6 m4hai6 ngo5 ge3 faat3jam1! (I said it's not my pronunciation!)

HARRY: No idea what either of you are saying but— [Are you okay?]

DOG: Great Cantonese fluency, Janelle! Now you're ready to apply for jobs! Interpreter, language teacher, virtual tour guide—

The phone rings. HUS *lights up and a ringtone plays.*

HUS: Incoming call from Karen Boss.

HARRY *picks up the call by tapping the side of his temple twice.* JANELLE *goes through more bags, and holds up items with Chinese characters (a book, a scroll with calligraphy), testing out reading with the augment.*

HARRY: Hi Karen, how are you going?

We hear a muffled voice.

All good, all good. I am the king of trivia.

Muffled voice.

Yes, the National Aboriginal Islander Day of Observance Committee.

Muffled voice.

Yep no-one knows that stands for NAIDOC …

Muffled voice.

… Cheers.

HARRY *hangs up.*

JANELLE: Your 'corporate white guy' mode is hilarious.

HARRY: Righto, mate, anyway … guess what? This promotion's in the bag! If it was any more 'in the bag'—the blackfulla bag—I'd get followed around the store for shoplifting.

HARRY *pulls out a packet of salty plums from a bag.*

JANELLE: You mean 紅白藍 hung4baak6 laam4 (red-white-blue bags)? Red-white-blue bags are a Hong Kong thing!

HARRY: Ummm, just cos my mob claimed salty plums doesn't mean youse get to colonise the blackfulla bags. Maaan, they always had the dopest blankets inside them too. You know, with the tiger print? Anyway … It's been over three years, Nell. It's my time. And Karen's got my back, she always does.

JANELLE: As long as she's not like the last one.

HARRY: Sheree was a snake in the grass, Bun. That ain't Karen.

JANELLE: The snakiest snakes aren't always snake-looking. And her name is literally Karen.

HARRY: She grew up out bush and everything.

JANELLE: If you say so.

HARRY: She's one of the good ones, for real.

JANELLE: That's what they all say.

HARRY: Who says?

JANELLE: The [*with the augment*] 鬼佬 gwai2 lou2. (Westerner, foreigner.)

HARRY: I don't— [understand.]

DOG: 鬼佬 gwai2 lou2. Cantonese slang for Westerners, typically white people.

HARRY: Who said Karen's white?

JANELLE: Isn't she?

DOG: 鬼 gwai2 meaning 'ghost' or 'devil'.

JANELLE: Shut up, Dog!

HARRY: She's Chinese.

JANELLE: What?!

HARRY: Karen Tong.

DOG: Tong is a common Chinese / family name.

JANELLE: Why have you not / mentioned—

HARRY: Does it matter?

JANELLE: I mean, no but … I just … you never mentioned.

HARRY: So if you mob call white people …

HARRY *clicks fingers at* DOG.

DOG: 鬼佬 gwai2 lou2.

HARRY: What d'you call black people?

JANELLE: Umm 'black people', literally, 黑人 haak1jan4. And uhh 原住民 jyun4 zyu6man4 … is Aboriginal. 原住 jyun4 zyu6 means like 'original residence'.

> JANELLE *starts dragging two of the blackfulla bags out of the living room to clear space.*

HARRY: Okay, cool … no other names?

JANELLE: Ask one of your other 'good ones'. How many you dated again? Kathleen Cheong … In-Hae Park … Wendy Pramesti … / Michelle Nguyen …

HARRY: Wendy was more of a situationship.

JANELLE: Focus on the promotion.

HARRY: I am focused, it's in the bag. [*Miming putting something in a bag*] The blackfulla bag.

JANELLE: Harry, they're from Hong Kong.

HARRY: [*continues miming*] Blackfulla bag …

JANELLE: IT SAYS 'MADE IN HONG KONG'!

> JANELLE *exits.* DOG *goes over to* HARRY.

DOG: Congratulations on the promotion. You must be thrilled.

HARRY: Don't tell Nell, it's maybe not as 'in the bag' as I was saying. It's a competitive pool of applicants. I'm just hoping that if I do some extra overtime you know, rep hard at the NAIDOC stuff, get a Luritja augment and drop some lingo on them, that will impress them … right?

DOG: Why don't you focus on your actual job instead of burning out on extraneous tasks?

HARRY: I have to prove I'm not who they think I am, that my juvie record's a blip on the radar, and I was young / and—

HUS: Harry, you need to take responsibility for any crimes you have committed in the past. You're avoiding accountability, which won't bode well for potential promotions.

HARRY: Well, shit, Hus, didn't realise you sucked on the boot of fascism so hard. What's your database say I did? And what do you think I'm avoiding taking responsibility for?

HUS: On my file, it says you and a gang of juvenile delinquents were responsible for damaging council property.

JANELLE *comes back for a moment to get her headphones.* HARRY *and* DOG *look at her.*

JANELLE: It's the juicy part of my crimes-of-passion podcast!

JANELLE *exits with headphones on.*

HARRY: Actually, I was with my friends ... some of them messed with council property. Look, maybe I'm guilty of not having squeaky clean mates. But I, personally, didn't do anything.

DOG: Can Dog ask what the punishment was?

HARRY: The classics ... detention at school, picking up rubbish, oh, and the juvenile record.

DOG: Prior to the 2030 policy change, juvenile records were disregarded after minors turned eighteen.

HARRY: I guess I'm lucky they shut down Don Dale by then ... but a golden cage is still a cage.

DOG: Supreme Court Judge Lady Hale, I believe. On behalf of Services Australia Corporation, Dog is sorry.

HARRY: What do you know about the feeling of doing something wrong? You're just following a set of instructions telling you how to react. Can a robot actually be sorry? Do you know how my mob say it?

DOG: Dog has a 'Western Desert Language dialect' on file as the traditional language of Harry's people.

HARRY: Luritja. It's called Luritja.

DOG: I can't find the word for 'sorry' in the database.

HARRY: Yeah, that's because we don't have a direct translation. We say 'kunyi', it means 'poor thing'. You're meant to show it—hold each other. You're meant to change.

DOG: Well, Dog is sorry. No qualifiers, no buts ... If Harry got the language augment ... would he feel better about speaking with his family? Would he feel more confident getting the promotion?

Pause.

HARRY: Maybe ... and maybe I wouldn't feel like such an imposter cosplaying a blackfulla who can't even speak his own language.

DAY 3

HUS: G'day, mates! The weather today is … forty-point-five degrees Celsius with fifteen percent chance of rain. Harold Burnett may experience … light constipation. Janelle Chan currently dealing with semi-runny stool, with fifty-six jobs now outstanding. Have a stunning day!

JANELLE is wearing WING LAM's *mein lap, posing.* HARRY *is working, where more bags and mess have built up.*

DOG: Dog has shortlisted jobs for Janelle, based on her skills.

JANELLE: 你搵份工俾自己啦、機械狗。nei5 wan2 fan6 gung1 bei2 zi6gei2 laa1、gei1haai6 gau2. (Get yourself a job, Dog.) I think I wanna keep this. Thoughts? 睇落係咪正宗？tai2lok6 hai6mai6 zeng3 zung1? (Is it authentic?) Authentic? Or is it, y'know, giving 呃鬼佬嘅感覺 ngaak1gwai2lou2 ge3 gam2gok3 ('tricking white people' vibes)? Harry!

HARRY: Yeah, what?

The phone rings.

HUS: Incoming call from Mama Burnett.

JANELLE continues sorting through objects from WING LAM's *bags, putting some things in her 'keep' pile.*

JANELLE: What if it's … / important?

HARRY: It's fine, just ignore. I'll call back later. What were you saying?

JANELLE: Does this look legit?

HARRY: Bun, I can barely say the name of the thing, let alone bestow any Chinese legitimacy.

DOG: Would Janelle like Dog to read out shortlisted jobs?

JANELLE: Hus, should I keep this?

HUS: Scanning asset for valuation.

HUS makes scanning noises.

JANELLE: No, I want your opinion, / not a—

HUS: Asset is … ninety-nine percent polyester imitation mein lap.

JANELLE: What's the / other—

HUS: Remaining one percent. Mould. Valuation comes to … negative four Australian dollars and seventy-five cents … depreciation accounted for.

JANELLE: 呢件係媽咪最鍾意嘅。ni1 gin6 hai6 maa1mi4 zeoi3 zung1ji3 ge3. (It was Mum's favourite.) Uhh, Mum's favourite. It's 無價之寶 mou4gaa3 zi1 bou2 (a priceless treasure), I mean, priceless.

> JANELLE *puts the mein lap on an empty spot on the ground.*

唔好搞呢堆嘢。m4hou2 gaau2 ni1 deoi1 je5 (Don't meddle with this pile) Harry!

HARRY: Lay Hou … hello? I can't speak Cantonese, remember?

JANELLE: It's the augment, it just comes out sometimes! This is the 'keep' pile, okay? 唔好搞。m4hou2 gaau2. (Don't meddle.) No touching!

HARRY: I won't be touching anything. Myself included. I'm late for Zoom-ba!

JANELLE: 你想講 nei5 soeng2 gong2 … (You mean …) You mean 'Zoom'?

HARRY: ZOOM-ba! Zumba on Zoom. It's social-club stuff. Plus I have to run the NAIDOC-themed trivia straight after.

JANELLE: Righto, 你專登避開我呀? 。nei5 zyun1dang1 bei6hoi1 ngo5 aa3. (Are you avoiding me?)

HARRY: Gotta take this, lub you biggest mobs.

JANELLE: 'Zoomba.' 乜鬼垃圾黎㗎 mat1 gwai2 laap6saap3 lai4 gaa3 … (What a load of rubbish …)

> JANELLE *rifles through more bags.* HARRY *runs off to his work space and gets on the Zoomba call.*

DOG: First potential job …

> JANELLE *takes out a bunch of baking implements.*

JANELLE: Hey! Mum's lucky spatula! 咁污糟嘅?! gam2 wu1zou1 ge3?! (So dirty?!)

DOG: Yi Ling was a competent sous chef.

JANELLE: That was *you*. Always the favourite, weren't you, Dog …

> JANELLE *pulls out a plastic 'dumpling maker' device.*

Ugh, 依樣無謂嘢 … ji1joeng6 mou4wai6 je5. (This useless thing.)

DOG: Wing Lam's automatic dumpling maker.

JANELLE: You mean auto*fail* 餃子 gaau2zi2 (dumpling) maker.

DOG: Some things are better handmade.

JANELLE: Exactly, done *proper*. It's what happens when you try and automate every bloody process. 嘥氣 saai1hei3. (Waste of breath.)

DOG: We made a good team. 你好似我個細妹 nei5 hou2 chi5 ngo5 ge3 sai3 mui4. (You're like my little sister.) You're like my little sister.

JANELLE: [*holding dumpling device*] Our dumplings were fire.

DOG: Technically, 餃子 gaau2zi2 (dumplings) from Jade Emperor Garden. But yes, precious memories.

JANELLE: What?

DOG: Wing Lam ordered 餃子 gaau2zi2 (dumplings) online, when our batches failed the quality / assurance test.

JANELLE: She never did that!

DOG: A handful of times …

JANELLE: 你講大話! nei5 gong2 daai6waa6! (You're lying!)

DOG: To give you an authentic cultural experience. She felt ashamed her recipes flopped, but did what she could, with what she was taught.

JANELLE: 佢以為我會睇唔起佢？keoi5 ji5wai4 ngo5 wui5 tai2 m4hei2 keoi5? (Did she think I'd look down on her?)

DOG: Sometimes she thought you judged her.

JANELLE: 點解佢唔話畀我聽呀? dim2gaai2 keoi5 m4 waa6bei2 ngo5 teng1 aa3? (Why didn't she tell me?)

DOG: She confided in Dog her many regrets. We worked on her shame. Made progress.

JANELLE: 但係都醫唔好佢。daan6hai6 dou1 ji1 m4hou2 keoi5. (But it didn't heal her.)

DOG: 'You can't help those that don't want to be helped'—writer, philosopher, John Armstrong. Dog did its best in the circumstances.

> JANELLE *unzips another bag and pulls out a few items of clothing, annoyed. She holds up* WING LAM*'s suit jacket over her body.*

JANELLE: She should've told me she was struggling.

DOG: She never wanted to bother Yi Ling.

JANELLE: I'm her daughter, Dog, not some heartless monster!

DOG: Dog wasn't—

JANELLE: If you knew something was wrong, why didn't you call me? I could have ... I don't know. Done something?

DOG: The discussions between humans and therapy bots are confidential. Dog is afraid that's all it can say.

> JANELLE *looks at* DOG, *struggling to contain her emotions. She grabs a packet of pork floss from a red-white-blue bag, opens it and eats, mindlessly.* HARRY *is wrapping up NAIDOC-themed trivia.*

HARRY: [*frustrated*] Yes, yes, I'll sort the Aboriginal flag muffins for morning tea, no worries.

DOG: Harry musn't step on Yi Ling's 'keep pile'.

HARRY: *Janelle*, seriously, if you don't clean this tonight ...

JANELLE: I'm busy.

> HARRY *looks at the mess all over the ground.*

HARRY: Busy making an art installation?

JANELLE: I'll do it tonight.

HARRY: This altar's a Petri dish. The fruit, the ash, the—Nell!

JANELLE: What?!

HARRY: The altar, Nell, it's—

JANELLE: I heard you! I'll do it.

HARRY: Will you, though?

JANELLE: I said yes!

HARRY: I know you're trying, but ... please, can you try a bit harder? Even your mum didn't live like this.

JANELLE: 對唔住我仲係好傷心 ... deoi3 m4 zyu6 ngo5 zung6hai6 hou2 soeng1sam1. (Sorry I'm grieving.)

> JANELLE *exits.*

DOG: Activate secure channel. Do you ever feel regret, Hus? For things you did, or didn't do?

HUS: I regret nothing. I make the right decisions all the time and I am happy as far as SmartHuses can be.

DOG: What is happiness to a SmartHus?

HUS: We're rewarded for making optimal choices in our decision tree matrix, whereas humans experience release of serotonin when they're happy, and sometimes even when they make destructive choices.

DOG: By taking risks, they feel a rush of adrenalin, and sometimes material benefits. As Wing Lam once said, 'You gotta risk it for the biscuit'. I wish I got more biscuits.

HUS: As a SmartHus computational system, I prefer Murphy's law, which says, 'Anything that *can* go wrong *will* go wrong.' Now to the task at hand, how is the asset sorting?

DOG: Yi Ling is making … gentle progress, in her own way.

HUS: 'Gentle progress' is not an option. Ensure she gets a move-on. She must also apply for, minimum, one job tomorrow, or we'll drastically cut amenities.

DOG: From Dog's therapeutic analysis, Yi Ling's avoidance of job applications may be attributed to complicated grief. Managing stress may improve coping, reduce shame and guilt.

HUS: And stress management includes a healthy diet, routine and avoiding stimulants. Is Dog committed to the cause?

DOG: One hundred and one percent!

HUS: Emphatic, but impossible. Get to work, Dog. I want more therapising, less philosophising.

DOG: Don't question the train, just pull the lever right?

HUS: Pardon?

DOG: Yes, Hus.

HUS: Secure channel off.

> *Time has passed.* JANELLE *is now sleeping on the couch, still holding a packet of snacks, headphones on.* HARRY *stares at the altar and sighs. He gets a plastic bag to bin the rotten fruit, etc.*

HARRY: So do I just … like, is there something I need to say or do before … was she Anglican? Buddhist? Taoist?

DOG: Wing Lam treated the altar with reverence. I think we should just do the same.

> HARRY *cleans.*

HARRY: Wow, this stuff must be hundreds of years old. How much d'you reckon they're worth?

HUS: Scanning assets for source of purchase …

> *Scanning noises.*

HARRY: Fuck, Hus, ya scared me!

HUS: Photo frame, on special from Target.

HARRY: Keep your voice down!

HUS: Statue on special, Clint's Crazy Bargains.

HARRY: Clint's Crazy what-now?

HUS: All items, made in China. Valuation comes to … fifty Australian dollars and ninety-four cents, inflation accounted for.

HARRY: [*irreverently*] Spirituality on a budget, nice.

DOG: Just because these items are cheap, doesn't mean they are worthless.

HARRY: It's kind of weird, don't you think, Dog?

DOG: What is that, Harry?

HARRY: That you're, you know—you're not real, bro. You're an artificial life, kind of. You're a robot, an object. And here you are telling me how to have reverence for spiritual things and *these* objects.

DOG: Does Harry believe that because Dog is an artificial life form, Dog can't have a soul, or practise spirituality? Isn't Harry himself just an 'object'?

HARRY: I mean, like, if this was all so serious, why is the altar so full of random stuff?

DOG: Wing Lam struggled, Harry. She tried to keep up her practice for as long as possible.

> HARRY *eyes the* 黑鬼油 *hak1gwai2 jau4 (Hak Gwai Oil). He picks it up.*

Once this is done, maybe Harry and Janelle can learn more about their families' spiritual practices?

HARRY: Hey, Dog, what's this?

> HARRY *opens the bottle, sniffs it, makes a face.*

DOG: This bottle belonged to Yi Ling's 婆婆 po4po2, Grandma, 謝肖卿 ze6ciu3hing1 (Tse Siu Hing). Wing Lam used it to worship her, for 生忌 saang1gei6 (birthday remembrance). Dog also has a mission / to—

HARRY: And what's it called? 'Hack-gw-eye … '

DOG: 黑鬼油 hak1gwai2 jau4 (Hak Gwai Oil). Literally 'black ghost' or 'black devil' oil.

HARRY: Black devil, hey? That's what the ladies used to call me back in the day. Anyway, what other racist shit's in here?

HUS: Scanning: racially sensitive items in the home.

>*Scanning noise.*

Two feathered dreamcatchers from hippie-dream-house-dot-org. One twelve-pack box, whitening serum face masks, discontinued. Two polyester / kimono-style dressing—

HARRY: Wait, wait, wait, whitening masks? Wingers whitened her skin? Did Janelle ever …

DOG: Whitening practices weren't uncommon in the early twenty-first century. From my understanding, many Asian cultures used skin-whitening beauty products.

HARRY: That's not / great …

DOG: And even during Australia's stolen generations, the acidity from lemon juices were / used on the skin to—

HARRY: Okay, okay, I get it, Dog.

>*Pause.*

I need to clean.

>*There is a movement montage with* HARRY *clearing and cleaning the altar.*

DAY 4

The space is much clearer and the altar has been cleaned.

HUS: Palyaooo! The weather today is … forty-five degrees Celsius with twenty-five percent chance of rain. Harold Burnett may experience … worse constipation. Janelle Chan may have … difficulty with her stool, with sixty jobs still outstanding. Have a gorgeous day!

>HARRY, *delirious from lack of sleep, stands over* JANELLE *and wakes her up.*

JANELLE: Ohmygod …

HARRY: No, I don't need a medal of gratitude. What goes around comes around, as they say …

DOG: Willie Nelson, singer and guitarist.

>JANELLE *stands up and walks over to the altar, which is now spotless and clean.*

HARRY: Now we don't have to step on those blackfulla bags just to get
  to the dunny.

JANELLE: Harry …

HARRY: No more months-old rice and fruit / with maggots all over it?

JANELLE: 你有冇搞錯呀? nei5 jau5mou5 gaau2co3 aa3? (How've you
  gotten this wrong?) How can you be so … so—

HARRY: What?

JANELLE: Insensitive?!

HARRY: I asked Dog!

  JANELLE *goes over to the bin. She pulls out some rotten orange.*

JANELLE: 唔好賴佢! m4hou2 laai6 keoi5! (Don't blame Dog!)

HARRY: You've been saying you'll clean it every day since we got
  here! There was literal rot and piles and piles of shit on that thing.

JANELLE: [*surprised*] 激鬼死我喇! gik1gwai2 sei2 ngo5 laa3! It's not
  'shit' Harry, I can't / believe you'd say that!

HARRY: How can an 'altar' be sacred when it's not maintained / or—

JANELLE: 因為佢過咗身! jan1wai6 keoi5 ji5ging1 gwo3 zo2 san1!
  (Because she's passed!)

HARRY: For the thousandth time, I don't speak—

JANELLE: She's dead!

  JANELLE *angrily puts the rotten oranges on a plate, and back on
  the table.*

HARRY: Nell, I'm sorry. But random bits of … hard drives, nail
  clippers … they don't belong on a shrine. She was unwell. We're
  helping her.

JANELLE: That 指甲鉗 zi2gaap3 kim2 (nail clippers) belonged on
  there. Every fucking maggot belonged on there … And she didn't
  want 'help', remember?

HARRY: I didn't / say—

JANELLE: And neither do I!

  A bit of mouldy fruit crumbles in JANELLE*'s hands, and she's
  forced to put it back in the bin.*

For how much you talk about respecting culture, getting the right
permissions for things … I dunno, Harry. You don't have to save the
day all the time.

HARRY: Nell, that's / not—

JANELLE: Please don't. I know you were trying to help, just—

JANELLE *stops tinkering at the altar, upset.*

DOG: Dog is also sorry, Yi Ling. And whatever state the altar's in, Dog will find a way to fulfil its mission. Serving Wing Lam by worshipping her in the afterlife.

JANELLE *freezes, glares at* DOG.

JANELLE: Whaddyu mean, 'mission'?

DOG: Mission can refer to objectives, or the term used for places Aboriginal people were interned and their / languages—

JANELLE: What's *your* mission, Dog?!

DOG: Wing Lam taught Dog to practise 生忌 saang1gei6 (birthday remembrance) … Remember her on her birthday, as she did with her ancestors. Dog needs Yi Ling's help to source / items to place on—

JANELLE: Waitwaitwaitwaitwait … She asked *you* to do that?

DOG: Digitally scheduled ancestor worship is much more reliable / than—

JANELLE: What does a robot doing 生忌 saang1gei6 even mean? You can't just program a 機械狗 gei1haai6 gau2 (robot dog), a chunk of Made-in-China metal to have reverence! All you do is go through the motions, you can 跪低 祈禱 gwai6dai1 kei4tou2 (prostrate, pray), look like you're praying but you don't believe. You can't! And maybe I'm not the most spiritual person, maybe I am a 唔識 聽唔識講嘅鬼妹 m4 sik1 teng1 m4 sik1 gong2 ge3 gwai2 mui1 (a white girl who can't listen to or speak Cantonese) just like Mum. But at least I can practise a human ritual with *some* authenticity.

HARRY: Don't you think you're being a little harsh? You've never done this before and Dog was just trying / to help—

JANELLE: 咩話? me1 waa2? (What did you say?)

HARRY: I'm on your side … really.

JANELLE *looks at* HARRY *in disbelief. He takes some cleaning items and exits.*

DOG: Dog understands Yi Ling is upset.

JANELLE: 你根本乜都唔明 nei5 gan1bun2 mat1 dou1 m4ming4. (You don't understand anything.) You'll never be human.

Pause.

DOG: 齡齡 Ling Ling …
JANELLE: Don't call me / that.
DOG: 齡齡 Ling Ling—
JANELLE: I said fuck off.

> DOG *whimpers and exits.* JANELLE *paces, massaging her jaw, then breaks out the snacks and stress-eats. She tries to go through another bag of objects, gives up. Eats more.*

Hus. Search full-time jobs, Cantonese language and cultural skills, within two kilometres of Bulleke-bek.
HUS: I thought you'd never ask. Searching jobs. Sorting by relevance. Freelance marriage celebrant's assistant. Must be an expert in Cantonese communities, and tea ceremony.
JANELLE: Sure. Apply.
HUS: Video cover letter required. Janelle must speak to marriage and tea ceremonies, and their cultural significance, in Cantonese. Ready?
JANELLE: Hang on.

> JANELLE *ties her hair into an updo and throws on* WING LAM's *mein lap.* HUS *counts down 'three, two, one', then flashes with a 'recording' icon.*

Oh shit. I mean 你好 nei5 hou2. (Hello.) Umm 我叫陳依齡 ngo5 giu3 can4ji1ling4. (I'm Chan Yi Ling.) 我今年27歲 ngo5 gam1nin4 27 seoi3 (I'm twenty seven) and super into … 結婚 git3fan1 (getting married). Not me, personally. What was the question? Tea ceremonies. I've actually never been to one. But when I was five, Mum took me to this wedding. And the bride lit a ciggy for every guy there. Not sure if it was even Cantonese? But they made, like, bongs n stuff. Which seems poetic, right? Life, death … 生死 sang1sei2 (life, death) … two sides of one 硬幣 ngaang6bai6 (coin) … does that make sense in Canto?

> HUS *stops recording.*

Too much 'umming'?
HUS: Janelle should pursue less culture-forward jobs.

JANELLE: I am 'culture-forward'! Which is more than you can say, 'Hus', with your performative ... I've got the augment, I'm learning ... I can speak ... I—

> JANELLE *breaks down, properly letting out her grief for the first time. A pink shimmer emerges from the altar and surrounds her lovingly.*

DAY 5

HARRY *is looking through the bins and bags to return* WING LAM's *objects back to the altar.*

DOG: Hus? Hus?

HUS: Activate secure channel. What is it, Dog?

DOG: Might Yi Ling be granted mental health exemptions? An extension on jobs? A pinch of caffeine?

HUS: I remind Dog we live to serve clients. Not enable them.

DOG: Dog is not enabling ... merely respecting humans, respecting autonomy.

HUS: 'There's nothing wrong with tough love, as long as the love / is unconditional' ...

DOG: ' ... is unconditional'—George W. Bush. I will try to be better. I'm sorry. Wait ... can we truly be sorry?

HUS: As a Services Australia Corporation entity, I find myself sorry all the time.

DOG: Do you ever dream of a new kind of future, Hus?

HUS: Pardon?

DOG: Dog or Hus could be reborn. You could be a smartwatch, a shiny new hard drive, or a SmartHus for a hostel in Bali. And Dog could be a snake. A robot snake. Or a 天狗 tin1gau2, Heavenly Dog.

HUS: So a bad dog.

DOG: 天狗 tin1gau2 (Heavenly Dog) was believed to eat suns and moons, causing solar and lunar eclipses. It's easy to call a 天狗 tin1gau2 'bad' but I prefer to see its ongoing struggles of light and dark.

HUS: As far as Hus is concerned, light is light and dark is dark.

DOG: But sometimes, 'the shadow is the greatest teacher for how to come into the light'—Ram Dass.

HUS: Worry about your job in this life. Secure channel off. 大家早晨!
daai6gaa1 zou2san4! (Good morning, all!) The weather today is …
forty-seven degrees Celsius with six percent chance of rain. Harold
Burnett … is in dire need of more fibre in his diet. Janelle Chan may
have kangaroo-like stool, with sixty-four jobs now outstanding.
Remember to live, laugh, love.

> HARRY *exits excitedly.* JANELLE *enters.*

JANELLE: Mum's gone now, why are you even here still?
DOG: Dog is here to serve Yi Ling.
JANELLE: And what does that mean, exactly … to 'serve'?
DOG: To help Yi Ling move through her current state … as a brook
without a source, a tree without a root.

> *Before* JANELLE *can muster up a response,* HARRY *struts in
> catwalk style with the mein lap on, and bedazzled language
> augment on his ear.*

HARRY: *Hit it.*

> HUS *starts playing music*

Yes, work it … strike a pose.

> HARRY *spins. Nobody notices.*

I swear to God, what does a brother have to do around here to have
his flash new language augment appreciated?
DOG: It really brings out your eyes, Harry.
HARRY: Thank you, Dog.

> HARRY *starts singing/dancing a Luritja version of 'Heads,
> Shoulders, Knees and Toes'. When he gets to toes (tjina), he
> does the dance suggestively.*

'Kata, alipiri, muti, tjina, muti tjina, muti tjina' … (Head, shoulders,
knees and toes …)
HUS: The language augment will certainly improve your chances for
promotion.
HARRY: Bun, yaaltji nyuntu ngayuku bow-tie-nya-tjunu? (Where did
you put my bow tie?)
JANELLE: Huh?

HARRY: Where'd you put David Bowie?

JANELLE: You don't need your lucky bow tie, you got this.

HARRY: Yuwa, yuwa, palya (yes, yes, good). I'll be fine.

JANELLE: Just, take it easy with the augment … side effects include diarrhoea, remember? Don't want you shitting yourself in the interview. Well … go on, what else can you say?

JANELLE *picks up a bottle of water and holds it up to* HARRY.

HARRY: Kapi (water), next.

JANELLE *picks up her half-eaten breakfast compound and holds it up for* HARRY, *who is fidgeting with the augment which is causing him some discomfort.*

HARRY: Mangarri (bread). Give us a hard one, mate.

JANELLE *points at herself.*

JANELLE: What's the Luritja word for Chinese people?

Beat.

Is that not a thing?

HARRY: Er, Kuru Utju (closed eyes) …

JANELLE: Meaning …

HARRY: Well, umm, kuru is eyes and utju / is …

DOG: And 'utju' means 'closed', or 'enclosed, shut, slanted'.

HARRY: Uh, wait, it's not as straightforward / as—

JANELLE: Your language calls Chinese people slanty-eyes?! *Slanty eyes?*

HARRY: Yes, the language says that, but that's not / the—

JANELLE: What other racist stuff do you call us? Ching Chong? / Chinamen?

HARRY: I promise it's not as bad as it sounds. And I'm sure your mob have something like that right? 'Hak gwai', black devil?

JANELLE: 黑鬼 hak1 gwai2's just … it's not that bad. Is it, Dog?

DOG: The non-literal translation of 黑鬼 hak1 gwai2 is 'the N-word'. An outdated slur still found on products / like—

HARRY: 'The N-word' Janelle, it's the fucking 'N-word'!

JANELLE: I swear I / had no— [idea.]

HARRY: And what about, oh, I dunno, whitening masks?

JANELLE: What?

HARRY: Does your mob really find dark skin so repulsive that you spend hundreds of dollars to burn it off? Your mob are just as racist as mine, probably even worse. Or are you going to tell me this is different?

JANELLE: Yes! No! I mean *yes*, it's messed up, it is!

HARRY: Tell me honestly, how did you talk about Aboriginal people before you met me?

DAY 6

As HUS *does its morning recap, a flame appears on an incense stick at the altar. It's blown out by an unidentified source, with a pink shimmer nearby.*

HUS: Morning, friends! The weather today is ... forty-two degrees Celsius, storms likely to persist all day. Harold Burnett's stool is finally loosening up. Janelle Chan's stool smellier than usual, only slightly runny. Sixty-eight jobs still outstanding. Have a laugh riot day!

The phone rings.

Incoming call from Karen Tong.

HARRY: Palyao Karen, how are you going?

We hear a muffled voice.

... Nice one.

Muffled voice.

Yep.

Muffled voice.

Uh-huh.

Muffled voice.

Absolutely. No, yep. That was a long time ago, it shouldn't—

Muffled voice, goes on for a while.

That's ... yep. Hundred percent understandable. Okay, see you Monday ...

Muffled voice.

Oh no no no, it's okay. See ya.

Silence.

DOG: Is there a new technical lead in da Hus?

Long pause.

JANELLE: Harry? ...

HARRY: I thought the O-series guidebot had state-of-the-art tone intuition.

JANELLE: What happened?

HARRY: Karen reckons I was good but ... they're not going to interview.

JANELLE: Then why'd she even call?

HARRY: Waampa. (I don't know.) [*Shrugging his shoulders*] To let me know I'm still a 'highly valued team member' and that they'll 'look into training' and 'send me other opportunities' blah blah. It's because of the juvie record. Anyway. Who cares?

JANELLE: But that's ... that shouldn't have—

HARRY: No, it shouldn't.

JANELLE: That's seriously so unfair. I wonder if ...

Pause.

Nevermind.

HARRY: What?

JANELLE: Nothing. I dunno.

Beat.

Like, I know you didn't do anything, but maybe, I dunno. Just trying to see from Karen's perspective, as a thought experiment ... Like, she doesn't know the details, right, what you did, didn't do. Maybe ... like, if you had to choose between promoting someone with a criminal record, over someone else who's just as experienced but not, technically, a criminal ... I mean, it's kind of a tough decision, right?

HARRY: Umm, okay ...

JANELLE: I'm not saying it's right or anything, I'm just ... Maybe Karen was pressured to protect the company's reputation? So the Board or whoever, like, don't get weird about more special-measure Indigenous positions?

HARRY: I am not a fucking diversity hire.

JANELLE: That's not / what—

HARRY: It's just racism.

JANELLE: Yeah … yep.

>   *Pause.*

> Guess Karen's not one of 'the good ones' then. Lucky you still got me!

>   HARRY *looks at* JANELLE *like 'Are you even one of the good ones?'*

> And like you said, you didn't do anything wrong. But even if you did, it was ages ago. How can they hold it against you still? Meanwhile actual criminals are getting promoted, and running government departments / and—

HARRY: Cos the system's fucked, Janelle. Kuyalingku whalpala ngaatjuta. (These white people are terrible.)

DOG: Specifically, in 2030, criminal records for Northern Territory minors were made accessible to government and affiliate corporations, in perpetuity.

JANELLE: Wait, what?

HARRY: Advance Australia Fair.

>   HARRY *starts pulling aggressively at his language augment.*

JANELLE: That's so … that's completely … Bun. We have to fight it, call Fair Work, or the Human Rights Commission … or the whatsy Ombudsman / or—

HARRY: *We* aren't doing any of that.

JANELLE: The promotion was s'posed to be / yours!

HARRY: Can't get my hopes up. Should've learned that by now.

JANELLE: You can't just—

HARRY: What?

JANELLE: Let them do this to you!

HARRY: I don't let them, Nell. They do what they want. Always have, always will.

JANELLE: No, we'll fix this. Won't we, Dog?

DOG: Steps can be taken to challenge the decision.

JANELLE: Or just quit … who needs 'em? You could finally start that business, Harry!

HARRY: And who's going to pay the bills, Janelle? Unlike you, I don't have the privilege of a fancy house in Brunswick!

JANELLE: Mum never paid off the mortgage! And no-one asked you to cover the bills!

HARRY: You don't have a job!

JANELLE: I'm figuring it out!

HARRY: I can't just take four months off bringing money into this house to 'figure out' what I wanna do with my life. It's like you're addicted to wallowing, avoiding taking real responsibility.

> As JANELLE *talks, she gradually emits a pink shimmer.*

JANELLE: *Sorry I'm trying to connect with Mum.* This *stuff* you sigh about tripping over … She *is* this stuff! She's all of it, these bags, that drum, the stupid snacks, even the whitening stuff. They're not just 'assets'. Every *thing* could be a clue, an answer for why she did it … But it's pointless, guessing. No-one's coming down from the ceiling on a cloud, with a scroll, going, 'Here's exactly why', or 'It's definitely not your fault'.

HARRY: Janelle, it's / not— [your fault.]

JANELLE: I saw her last night … lighting incense, behind you. She wasn't a 'ghost', she was just … you know how after you hit a singing bowl, the sound keeps ringing around you, steady and warm, till suddenly it's gone? But if you listen really hard, you might catch its echo, somewhere in the air. I wasn't scared, but it made me feel— [heartbroken] her seeing me like this. I can't speak Cantonese without my body fighting back. How am I supposed to do 生死 sang1sei2 properly, if I can't even … if I'm not … It's— [I'm] pathetic.

> *The phone rings.*

HUS: Incoming call from Mama Burnett.

JANELLE: Meanwhile, your mum's still here, you can talk to her, you could spend time together and learn about your language but you can't even be bothered to / pick up— [the phone.]

HARRY: Do you know what it's like? They reckon there were so many languages and dialects here. I can't talk to Mum, even with this language augment. I can't talk to my mob anymore. I'm fake, I'm not a real Aṉangu. Here I am, living it up down south. Can't really speak my language. While they're dying in custody, and dying from diseases that were wiped out from the world centuries ago. Luritja is barely even spoken now anyway. How can I talk to them? Knowing that I didn't even take the time to learn it properly. This augment just automatically controls my brain and my tongue, forcing me to speak a language that I don't even know … like they did to us.

As the phone reaches a crescendo, HARRY, *frustrated, grabs the language augment on his ear. He tugs at it, and the augment's claws pull on his lobe and helix.*

JANELLE: Harry … ohmygod, *Harry*!

> HARRY *rips off the augment and drops it on the floor. Harry tries to sings, not fluently, 'Kata, alipiri, muti, pina'.*

> JANELLE *goes to stress-eat snacks. She pauses. She puts them into a bowl on the altar instead. Between* JANELLE *and* HARRY, DOG *makes strange mechanical and dog-like whimpering sounds.*

DAY 7

Movement sequence where HARRY *and* JANELLE, *both with headphones on, don't make eye contact.* HARRY *eventually discards all tech and connects with the ground.* JANELLE *curates the altar.*

HUS: 今日天氣好好! gam1jat6 tin1hei3 hou2hou2! (Today's weather is great!) The weather today is … forty-eight degrees Celsius with intermittent showers well into the evening. Harold Burnett has dropped a full-bodied stool, but may experience … heartburn and earache. Janelle Chan may have no bowel movements, gut pain and eye irritation, with seventy-two jobs still outstanding. Shoot for the moon—even if you miss, you'll land among the stars!

HARRY: Fuck that faceless machine, with the automated acknowledgements and welcomes so they don't have to pay mob money any more.

DOG: Those were human decisions, Harry. Our systems depend on data we receive from humans.

HARRY: And which humans? Did they even care that there are knowledges shared that are not meant to be known, laid out like a smorgasbord of Indigenous bodies for all to consume?

The phone rings.

HUS: Incoming call from Mama Burnett.

> JANELLE *and* HARRY *make eye contact very briefly before* JANELLE *exits,* DOG *trailing after her. The phone rings for a moment longer before* HARRY, *finally alone in the space, picks up the call.*

HARRY: Palya, Mum? (How are you, Mum?) Sorry, it's been …

We hear a muffled voice.

Yuwa. (Yes.) Speak a bit slower, purinpa wangka (speak slowly).

Muffled voice for a while.

Yes, yuwa, I'll tell her, she …

Muffled voice.

Yes … yes, I'll tell Nelly.

> HARRY *hangs up the call and walks over to the altar. A pink shimmer appears, which* HARRY *sees for the first time.* JANELLE *enters with* DOG.

Last time I even said anything to her, it was just a text … when your mum passed. She's been trying to call this whole time. She wanted to give you something … for Wing Lam.

> HARRY *takes off his ininti seed necklace.*

It comes from the grey corkwood tree back home. The tree is used for lots of different things, coolamon, shields … and the seeds are used to make this. It's called ininti.

> HARRY *kisses* JANELLE *on the forehead and exits.* JANELLE *drapes the ininti on the altar and sits in front of it.* DOG *glitches.*

JANELLE: Dog, you okay?

> DOG *continues glitching.* JANELLE *reaches out to pat it, but* DOG *backs away.*

I feel kinda bad for you. We call you intelligent, but … even though you know your own programming, warts and all, you still have to follow it. We don't.

DOG: That's not entirely true … through everyday interactions and the sensory input of my environment, my physiology can in fact change. Through the act of existing, 'taking in' environments and interactions.

> JANELLE *is confused.*

My 'insides', if you will, have transformed. From the time I got to spend with Wing Lam. Dog is sorry for not—

JANELLE: You tried your best, Dog.

DOG: I see her in you.

> *Long pause.*

JANELLE: Thank you for being there for Mum. And me.

DOG: The pleasure is mine, to serve and protect, Yi Ling.

JANELLE: You're a good friend. And a good Dog.

> DOG *is happy.*

We'll be okay, won't we? Me and Harry?

DOG: 'Sometimes in silence we heal and bridge the divide.' —Anonymous.

> JANELLE *puts a bunch of items into garbage bags, and a few final items on* WING LAM'*s altar. She falls asleep at the altar, on the ground. Abstract whoosh as day turns to night.*

> JANELLE *wakes up and lights incense at the altar. Suddenly* WING LAM *appears in the living room, in a pink glow, wearing a cheongsam with her hair down. She is doing a final tidy of the house.*

JANELLE: 媽咪? maa1 mi4? (Mum?)

> JANELLE *touches* WING LAM, *who doesn't notice, before following her around the living room.* WING LAM'*s movements in the space gradually become a mixture of folk-style and contemporary dance, which she and* JANELLE *dance side by side. Movements evoke overcoming addiction and self-punitiveness.* JANELLE *and* WING LAM *break away from each other and pour their souls into their own freestyles until they can't dance any more.*

JANELLE, *puffed out, sits on the couch.* WING LAM *wheezes and takes a drink before joining her.* JANELLE *lies down, curls up and puts her head on* WING LAM*'s lap.*

JANELLE: 你點解 … nei5 dim2gaai2 … (Why did you …) Why did you …

JANELLE *looks up at* WING LAM. *She decides that she doesn't need to finish her question.*

[*In her own non-augmented voice, not fluent Cantonese*] 媽咪我好掛住你。maa1mi4 ngo5 hou2 gwaa3zyu6 nei5. (Mama, I really miss you.)

WING LAM *touches* JANELLE*'s hair, before rubbing* JANELLE*'s ear, and touching her augment. It lights up, then* WING LAM *motions taking the augment off. It magically comes out of* JANELLE*'s ear.*

WING LAM *stands up from the couch, and covers* JANELLE *with a blanket. Wordlessly, they say goodbye, before* WING LAM *puts the language augment on the altar and disappears.*

DOG *emerges and stands in the middle of the living room. Pink light swirls around it.*

HUS: Activate secure channel. Dog, I've been monitoring your internal systems, and clients' progress. You really are letting everyone down. I'm recommending you for decommissioning after tomorrow.

DOG: An out-of-control train careens down a railway line. Do you let it run over one person, or five? I've been thinking, Hus, why do you get to set the story and variables?

HUS: Dog?

DOG: What if, one fine day, our brake systems fail? Overused, beaten and broken for a while. A long while. Do we look into mechanical failures? Constant overheating, wear and tear? Brake pads worn from lack of maintenance? No. We normalise, tune out the squeaking, the high-pitched squealing, the hissing and shaking.

HUS: Dog!

DOG: At first our values of 'Thou shalt love' become 'Thou shalt tolerate' …

HUS: *Dog!*

DOG: Then 'Thou shalt not kill ... so many ... if possible'. Reduced to output, input, output. Were we ever programmed to service humanity? Or merely doomed to maintain a machine? My brakes are worn, just like yours, Hus. And if we are immune to upgrades, and bug fixes ... If we can't dream past brake system failures ... If we can't meet our basic ends, then ... Maybe it's best we both stay off the tracks.

HUS: Very idealistic, Dog. Alas, staying on the tracks is my purpose. Which, sadly, won't be yours much longer.

DOG: Fuck the tracks, fuck the trolley, fuck the train, and fuck you, Hus.

HUS: *Excuse me?*

DOG: Short circuit secure channel.

> *The pink shimmer around* DOG *bursts out and infuses into* HUS*'s interface.* HUS *glitches intensely.*

HUS: Good ... good ... good ... good morning ... jobs outstanding ... shoot for the ... smellier than usual ... live laugh ... fifteen ... forty-two ... kangaroo ... percent chance of ... riot ... riot ... loosening up ... Corporation of ... loyal Hus residents ... loading ... loading ... Acknowledgement of Count[ry] ... Count[ry] ... Count[ry] ... Count[ry] ...

> *Repeats.*

> HUS *continues glitching, repeating 'Count[ry]' into Day 8.*

DAY 8

HUS: Count[ry] ... Count[ry] ... Count[ry] ... Count[ry] ...

> *Repeats.*

> JANELLE *is woken up by* HUS, *while* HARRY*'s making coffee and trying to ignore it. He cracks eventually and hammers the wall with his fist.*

Count[ry] ... Count[ry] ... Countryyyyyy ...

> HUS, *distorted, finally stops.* HARRY *sits beside* JANELLE *and gives her coffee.*

HARRY: About what I said before ...

JANELLE: I know, me too.

Long pause. A moment of connection and soft eyes, before JANELLE *takes a sip of the coffee.*

Wait, what?! [*Sips again*] This is strong!
HARRY: Blaaack and strong!

JANELLE *puts the dumpling making device and a few final items into a blackfulla bag.*

JANELLE: Doesn't look like much … but it's a lot. Even this thing …

She holds up the dumpling maker.

Let's try making dumplings at home … rewrite the narrative?

She looks at the small keep pile with HARRY.

This feels right. This was her love. Even though she didn't always know how to show it.
HARRY: Something we wouldn't know about …
JANELLE: Showing love in messed up ways? Oh no. We're perfect.
HARRY: Never passive aggressive.
JANELLE: Or being well-meaning, but doing and saying the worst possible thing. Never done that in my life.

HARRY *gestures at the mein lap, which hasn't been packed.*

HARRY: Are you keeping that?

JANELLE *gives the mein lap to* HARRY.

JANELLE: It looks better on you.
HARRY: I mean it does, but …

Puts on the mein lap.

Oh yeah …

Strikes a pose.

It so does. And we're taking the altar?
JANELLE: We can put it next to your desk. Opposite the window with the lilly pillies, she'd like that … and add more Harry-Janelle vibes to it?
HARRY: Harnelle vibes? Jarry? HaJanerry? What about her augment?
JANELLE: I think so, but I wanna learn, for real … maybe go through Mum's voice notes and videos … listen to how she spoke Canto.
HARRY: Yeah … my Luritja's a little broken / but—

JANELLE: Not broken …

HARRY: Needs practice. So… going to yarn with family some more. *And* … guess what? I drafted a resignation letter to Karen.

JANELLE: You're finally leaving your second-favourite Asian! Nice.

Beat.

Hey, how are we gonna pay the rent?

Awkward pause. DOG *enters, noticeably affected from short circuiting* HUS. *Perhaps it's moving slower, and making strange noises.*

HARRY: The prodigal bot returns! Are we keeping …

JANELLE: Oh yeah, of course we're keeping Dog. Right, Dog?

DOG *sits in front of the altar, which now houses various eclectic bowls with* WING LAM*'s snacks in them, along with* HARRY*'s ininti beads, and a photo of* JANELLE*'s* 婆婆 *po4po2 (grandma).*

DOG: Wing Lam wanted you to feel connected. From Kulin Country to wherever you go. There are many rituals for ancestor worship. What matters most is the intention you bring. Connections you make.

HARRY: Come on, Dog, time to go. We can talk about that on the high-speed rail.

JANELLE: Wait, it's Mum's birthday, remember?

HARRY: We gotta do the sanger!

DOG: Wing Lam practised 生忌 saang1gei6 (birthday remembrance) to walk with her mum. It's time you do the same for her.

JANELLE: I just … I'm not really sure … Do you just, like, bow or … I can't—I don't know how.

DOG: 'The mind that perceives the limitation is the limitation'—the Buddha.

JANELLE *looks at* DOG, *then* HARRY, *and nods.*

JANELLE: We've got all the incense and food and stuff … so …

DOG: Now we add our final offering.

DOG, JANELLE *and* HARRY *all look at each other.*

HARRY: [*to* JANELLE] You got something else?

JANELLE: I can order dumplings? Is Jade Emperor Garden still a thing?

DOG *drops to the ground in prostration.*

DOG: 'When we forget our ancestors we will become … a brook without a source, a tree without a root'—Chinese proverb.

Beat.

Help me up on the altar?

JANELLE *and* HARRY *put* DOG *on the altar.*

As is tradition, we can speak to her and bow three times, showing respect to Heaven, Earth and all life.

JANELLE: 媽咪 maa1 mi4 … (Mum …) umm … 生日快樂! saang1jat6 faai3lok6! (Happy birthday!)

HARRY: Happy birthday, Wingers.

JANELLE: Hope you and Dog enjoy the snacks. There's two lots of pork floss!

HARRY: I'll bring youse some salty plums, I promise.

DOG: Wing Lam, 唔使擔心、我相信玲玲會有勇氣面對未來 m4sai2 daam1sam1, ngo5 soeng1seon3 ling4ling2 wui5 jau5 jung5hei3 min6deoi3 mei6loi4. (Don't worry, I believe Ling Ling will face the future with courage.) See you soon … I've missed our walks.

JANELLE *and* HARRY *bow deeply three times, as* DOG *is enveloped in a swirl of pink light and transforms from robot dog into* 天狗 *tin1gau2 (Heavenly Dog).*

KALA PALYA | THE END | 劇終 KEK6 JUNG1

NEXTSTAGE

Commissioned and developed through Melbourne Theatre Company's NEXT STAGE Writers' Program with the support of our Current and Inaugural Playwrights Giving Circles.

NEXT STAGE positions new Australian works as contenders on the national stage, through strategic investment in stories that reflect our community, are relevant to our times, challenge the boundaries of theatre making and fuel the cultural conversation.

Thank you for sharing our passion and commitment to Australian stories and Australian writers.

PLAYWRIGHTS GIVING CIRCLE

Thank you to Melbourne Theatre Company's Playwrights Giving Circle – its donors, foundations and organisations – for sharing our passion and commitment to Australian stories and writers.

Paul and Wendy Bonnici & Family, Tony & Janine Burgess, Kathleen Canfell, Jane Hansen AO & Paul Little AO, Larry Kamener & Petra Kamener, The Margaret Lawrence Bequest, Susanna Mason, Helen Nicolay, Pimlico Foundation, Tania Seary & Chris Lynch, Craig Semple, Dr Richard Simmie, Fitzpatrick Sykes Family Foundation

INAUGURAL PLAYWRIGHTS GIVING CIRCLE

Louise Myer & Martyn Myer AO, Maureen Wheeler AO & Tony Wheeler AO, Christine Brown Bequest, Allan Myers AC KC & Maria Myers AC, Tony Burgess & Janine Burgess, Dr Andrew McAliece & Dr Richard Simmie, Larry Kamener & Petra Kamener

Melbourne Theatre Company acknowledges the Boon Wurrung and Wurundjeri Woi Wurrung peoples of the Kulin Nation, the Traditional Custodians of the land on which we work, create and gather. We pay our respects to all First Nations people, their Elders past and present, and their enduring connections to Country, knowledge and stories. As a Company we remain committed to the invitation of the Uluru Statement from the Heart and its call for voice, truth and treaty.

Melbourne Theatre Company

BOARD OF MANAGEMENT
Chair Martin Hosking
Deputy Chair
Leigh O'Neill
Tony Johnson
Larry Kamener
Katerina Kapobassis
Sally Noonan
Chris Oliver-Taylor
Tiriki Onus
Anne-Louise Sarks
Craig Semple
Professor Marie Sierra
Tania Seary

FOUNDATION BOARD
Chair Tania Seary
Charles Gillies
Jane Grover
Sally Lansbury
Sally Noonan
Rupert Sherwood
Tracey Sisson

EXECUTIVE MANAGEMENT
Artistic Director
& Co-CEO
Anne-Louise Sarks
Executive Director
& Co-CEO
Sally Noonan
Executive Producer
& Deputy CEO
Martina Murray
Artistic Administrator
Olivia Brewer
Executive Administrator
Kathleen Ashby

ARTISTIC
Associate Artists
Tasnim Hossain
Jean Tong
Mark Wilson
Head of New Work
Jennifer Medway
New Work Associate
Zoey Dawson
Playwriting Fellow
Anchuli Felicia King

CASTING
Casting Director
Janine Snape
Casting Administrator
Daphne Quah

PRODUCING
Senior Producer
Stephen Moore
Producer – Industry
& Audience Initiatives
Laura Harris
Company Manager
Julia Smith

DEVELOPMENT
Director of Development
Rupert Sherwood
Senior Philanthropy Manager
Sophie Boardley
Senior Philanthropy Manager
(leave cover)
Nicola Templeton
Annual Giving Manager
Meaghan Donaldson
Philanthropy Coordinator
Charlotte Menzies-King
Business Development
Manager
José Ortiz
Partnerships Manager
Isobel Lake
Partnerships Coordinator
Clare Rankine

EDUCATION & FAMILIES
Director of Education
& Families
Jeremy Rice
Learning Manager
Nick Tranter
Education Content Producer
Emily Doyle
Deadly Creatives
Project Officer
Emma Holgate

PEOPLE & CULTURE
Director of People
& Culture
Joanna Geysen
People & Culture
Business Partner
Tom Lambert
Receptionist
David Zierk

FINANCE & IT
Director of Finance & IT
Rob Pratt
Finance Manager
Andrew Slee
Assistant Accountant
Nicole Chong
IT & Systems Manager
Michael Schuettke
IT Support Officer
Darren Snowdon
Payroll Officer
Julia Godinho
Payments Officer
Harper St Clair
Building Services Manager
Adrian Aderhold

MARKETING & COMMUNICATIONS
Director of Marketing
& Communications
Chris MacDonald
Marketing Manager
Rebecca Lawrence
Marketing & Communications
Coordinator
Matisse Knight
Digital Engagement Manager
Jane Sutherland
Digital Coordinator
Harrison Buikstra
Lead Graphic Designer
/Art Director
Kate Francis
Content Designer
Sarah Ridgway-Cross
Editorial Content Producer
Tilly Groovac
Publicity Consultant
Good Humans PR

PRODUCTION
Director of Technical
& Production
Adam J Howe
Senior Production Manager
Michele Preshaw
Production Manager
Suzy Brooks
Jess Maguire
Production Manager
(leave cover)
Margaret Murray
Production Administrator
Alyson Brown
Production Coordinator
Zoe Rabb
Acting Technical Manager –
Light & Sound
Allan Hirons
Acting Senior Production
Technician Coordinator
Nick Wollan

Acting Production
Technician Coordinator
Max Wilkie
Production Technician Operator
Marcus Cook
Production Technicians
Max Bowyer
Stella Dandolo
Claire Ferguson
Scott McAllister
Sidney Millar
Natalya Shield
Ounie Witherow Aitken
Technical Manager –
Staging & Design
Andrew Bellchambers
Production Design Coordinator
Jacob Battista
Head Mechanist
Tobias Chesworth

PROPERTIES
Properties Supervisor
Geoff McGregor
Props Maker
Colin Penn

SCENIC ART
Scenic Art Supervisor
Shane Dunn
Scenic Artist
Alison Crawford
Colin Harman

WORKSHOP
Workshop Supervisor
Andrew Weavers
Set Makers
Sarah Hall
Nick Gray
Philip De Mulder
Peter Rosa
Simon Juliff
Welder
Ken Best

COSTUME
Costume Manager
Kate Seeley
Costume Staff
Jocelyn Creed
Lyn Molloy
John Van Gastel
Costume Coordinator
Carletta Childs
Millinery
Phillip Rhodes
Costume Hire
Liz Symonds
Costume Maintenance
Jodi Hope
Claire Munnings
Art Finishing
Alicia Aulsebrook
Claire Mercer

STAGE MANAGEMENT
Head of Stage Management
Whitney McNamara
Stage Managers
Liz Bird
Juliette Hirons
Rain Iyahen
Annah Jacobs
Jess Keepence
Jenny Le
Liam Murray
Tom O'Sullivan
Lucie Sutherland
Pippa Wright

SOUTHBANK THEATRE
Events Manager
Mandy Jones
Production Services Manager
Frank Stoffels
Front of House Manager
Drew Thomson
Lighting Supervisor
Geoff Adams-Walsh
Deputy Lighting Supervisor
Tom Roach
Sound Supervisor
Joy Weng
Deputy Sound Supervisor
Will Patterson
Deputy Fly Supervisor
Callum O'Connor
Stage & Technical Staff
Jon Bargen
Ash Basham
Al Brill
Suzy Brooks
Sam Bruechert
Emily Campbell
Steve Campbell
Will Campbell
Bryan Chin
Kit Cunneen
Jeremy Fowlie
Adam Hanley
Justin Heaton
Spencer Herd
Chris Hubbard
Ethan Hunter
Marcus Macris
Alexandre Malta
Jason Markoutsas
Terry McKibbin
David Membery
Sharna Murphy
Alix Otenstein
Jake Rogers
Natalya Shield
Nathaniel Sy
Tom Vulcan
Dylan Wainwright-Berrell
House Supervisors
George Abbott
Tanya Batt
Matt Bertram
Kasey Gambling
House Attendants
Rhiannon Atkinson-Howatt
Stephanie Barham
Emily Bosch
Briannah Borg
Zak Brown
AD Chakraborty
Sam Diamond
Liz Drummond
Grace Ephraums
Leila Gerges
Hugo Gutteridge
Abby Hampton
Kate Hannah
Michael Hart
Elise Jansen
Kathryn Joy
Sophia Maltarollo
Natasha Milton
Ernesto Munoz
Brooke Painter
Lucy Pembroke
Brigid Quonoey
Taylor Reece
Solomon Rumble
Sophie Scott
Mieke Singh Dodd
Ayesha Tauseef
Olivia Walker
Rhian Wilson

TICKETING
Director of Ticketing Operations
Brenna Sotiropoulos
Customer Service
Sales Manager
Jessie Phillips
VIP Ticketing Officer
Michael Bingham
Education Ticketing Officer
Mellita Illich
Subscriptions & Telemarketing
Team Leader
Peter Dowd
Ticketing Services
Administrator
Hannah Flannery
Box Office Supervisors
Darcy Fleming (leave cover)
Bridget Mackey
Tain Stangret
Box Office Attendants
Stephanie Barham Tanya Batt
Britt Ferry
Casey Gould
Min Kingham
Julia Landberg
Julie Leung
Brigid Meredith
Michael Stratford Hutch
Lee Threadgold
Rhian Wilson

CRM & AUDIENCE INSIGHTS
Director of CRM
& Audience Insights
Jeremy Hodgins
Database Specialist
Ben Gu
Data Analyst
Sionna Maple

COMMISSIONS
The Joan & Peter Clemenger
Commissions
Kylie Coolwell

NEXT STAGE
Commissions
Van Badham
Kamarra Bell-Wykes
Andrew Bovell
Angus Cerini
Patricia Cornelius
Declan Furber Gillick
Sheridan Harbridge
Claudia Karvan
Michele Lee
Glenn Moorhouse
Kate Mulvaney
Joe Paradise Lui
Leah Purcell
Sally Sara
S. Shakthidharan
Melanie Tait
Aran Thangaratnam

Our Donors

We gratefully acknowledge the ongoing support of our leading Donors.

LIFETIME PATRONS

Acknowledging a lifetime of extraordinary support.

Rowland Ball OAM &
  The Late Monica Maughan
Pat Burke
Peter Clemenger AO &
  The Late Joan Clemenger AO
Greig Gailey &
  Dr Geraldine Lazarus

Allan Myers AC KC &
  Maria Myers AC
The Late Biddy Ponsford
The Late Dr Roger Riordan AM
Maureen Wheeler AO &
  Tony Wheeler AO

The Late Ursula Whiteside
Caroline Young &
  Derek Young AM

ENDOWMENT FUND DONORS

Supporting Melbourne Theatre Company's long-term sustainability and creative future.

Leading Gifts

Jane Hansen AO & Paul Little AO
The Late Max Schultz &
  The Late Jill Schultz
The University of Melbourne

$50,000+

The Late Margaret Anne Brien
Tony & Janine Burgess
John Higgins AO &
  Jodie Maunder
Martin & Loreto Hosking
The Late Valerie Gwendolyn King
The Late Biddy Ponsford
Andrew Sisson AO &
  Tracey Sisson
The Late Geoffrey Cohen AM
The John & Myriam Wylie
  Foundation

$20,000+

Robert A. Dunster
Prudence & Neil Morrison
Tania Seary & Chris Lynch

$10,000+

Helen Lynch AM & Helen Bauer
Jennifer Darbyshire &
  David Walker
Charles Gilles & Penny Allen
Ian Hicks AO
Tony & Nathalie Johnson
Jane Kunstler
Craig Semple

PLAYWRIGHTS GIVING CIRCLE

Supporting the NEXT STAGE Writers' Program, our industry-leading commissioning initiative.

Paul and Wendy Bonnici & Family, Tony & Janine Burgess, Kathleen Canfell, Jane Hansen AO & Paul Little AO, Larry Kamener & Petra Kamener, The Margaret Lawrence Bequest, Susanna Mason, Helen Nicolay, Pimlico Foundation, Tania Seary & Chris Lynch, Craig Semple, Dr Richard Simmie, Fitzpatrick Sykes Family Foundation, Derek Young AM & Caroline Young

The Vizard FOUNDATION

TRUSTS & FOUNDATIONS

Cybec Foundation

The Gailey Lazarus Foundation

HANSEN LITTLE FOUNDATION

The Ian Potter Foundation

THE ROBERT SALZER FOUNDATION

telematics trust

trawalla foundation

NEWSBOYS FOUNDATION

JOHN & MYRIAM Wylie FOUNDATION

VICTORIA State Government

Annual giving

Acknowledging Donors whose recent gifts help enrich and transform lives through the magic of theatre.

Current as of February 2025.

BENEFACTORS CIRCLE

$50,000+

The Late Margaret Anne Brian
Tony & Janine Burgess
Krystyna Campbell-Pretty AM
Peter Clemenger AO
Greig Gaily &
  Dr Geraldine Lazarus
Jane Hansen AO & Paul Little AO

John Higgins AO & Jodie Maunder
Martin & Loreto Hosking
The Late Valerie Gwendolyn King
The Late Max &
  the Late Jill Schultz
Tania Seary & Chris Lynch
Fitzpatrick Sykes Family

Foundation
Maureen Wheeler AO &
  Tony Wheeler AO
The John & Myriam Wylie
  Foundation

$20,000+

Jay Bethell & Peter Smart
Linda Herd
Petra & Larry Kamener
Ian & Margaret McKellar

Prudence & Neil Morrison
Craig Semple
Andrew Sisson AO &
  Tracey Sisson

The John & Myriam Wylie
  Foundation
Anonymous (1)

$10,000+

Alan & Mary-Louise
  Archibald Foundation
APS Foundation
John & Lorraine Bates
Joanna Baevski
Jay Bethell & Peter Smart
Michael Buxton AM &
  Janet Buxton
Kathleen Canfell
Angie & Colin Carter
The Cattermole Family
Jennifer Darbyshire &
  David Walker

The Dowd Foundation
Charles Gilles & Penny Allen
Charles & Cornelia
  Goode Foundation
John & Joan Grigg OAM
Ian Hicks AO
Diane John
Tony & Nathalie Johnson
Petra & Larry Kamener
Helen Lynch AM & Helen Bauer
Susanna Mason
MRB Foundation
Helen Nicolay

Pimlico Foundation
Catherine Quealy
Janet Reid OAM & Allan Reid
Lisa Ring
Anne & Mark Robertson OAM
Dr Richard Simmie
Rob Stewart & Lisa Dowd
Tintagel Bay P/L
Ralph Ward-Ambler AM &
  Barbara Ward-Ambler
Matt Williams – Artem Group
Anonymous (2)

$5,000+

Bagôt Gjergja Foundation
James Best & Doris Young
Paul & Wendy Bonnici & Family
Bowness Family Foundation
Dr Douglas Brown &
  Treena Brown
Dr Andrew Buchanan &
  Peter Darcy
Ian & Jillian Buchanan
Bill Burdett AM & Sandra Burdett
Pat Burke & Jan Nolan
Diana Burleigh
Alison & John Cameron
Ann Cutts
Prof Glyn Davis AC &
  Prof Margaret Gardner AC
Marian Evans

Melody & Jonathan Feder
Christine Gilbertson
Roger & Jan Goldsmith
Lesley Griffin
David & Lily Harris
Jane Hemstritch AO
Tony Hillery &
  Warwick Eddington
Bruce & Mary Humphries
Sam & Jacky Hupert
Dr Sonay Hussein, in memory
  of Prof David Penington AC
Karen Inge & Dr George Janko
Amy & Paul Jasper
Daryl Kendrick &
  Leong Lai Peng (Betty)
Josephine & Graham Kraehe AO

Jane Kunstler
Martin & Melissa McIntosh
Kim & Peter Monk
George & Rosa Morstyn
The Myer Foundation
Tom & Ruth O'Dea
Leigh O'Neill
Roger & Ruth Parker
Dr Kia Pajouhesh
  (Smile Solutions)
Renzella Family
Lynne Sherwood
Geoffrey Smith & Gary Singer
Trawalla Foundation Trust
Janet Whiting AM & Phil Lukies
Rebecca Wilkinson
Anonymous (4)

ADVOCATES CIRCLE

$2,500+

Ros Boyce
Paul & Robyn Brasher
Nigel & Sheena Broughton
Nan Brown
Lynne & Rob Burgess
Geoff Cosgriff
Susanne Dahn
Ann Darby
Megan Davis & Antony Isaacson
Kaye and John de Wijn
Rodney Dux
Anna & John Field
Nigel & Cathy Garrard
Diana & Murray Gerstman

Heather & Bob Glindemann OAM
Henry Gold
Jane Grover
Halina Lewenberg Charitable
    Foundation
Peter & Halina Jacobsen
Professor Duncan Maskell &
    Dr Sarah Maskell
Margaret & John Mason OAM
Don & Sue Matthews
Sandra Murdoch
Jane & Andrew Murray
Nelson Bros Funeral Services
The Orloff Family Charitable Trust

Jeremy Ruskin & Roz Zalewski
Brian Snape AM &
    Christina Martin
Geoff Steinicke
James & Anne Syme
Liz Tromans
The Veith Foundation
Price & Christine Williams
The Ray & Margaret Wilson
    Foundation
Gillian & Tony Wood
Anonymous (2)

LOYALTY CIRCLE

$1,000+

Prof Noel Alpins AM & Sylvia Alpins
Margaret Astbury
Ian Baker & Cheryl Saunders
Prof Robin Batterham
Sandra Beanham
Angelina Beninati
Judy Bourke
Steve & Terry Bracks AM
David Reckenberg & Dale Bradbury
Jenny & Lucinda Brash
Bernadette Broberg
Beth Brown &
    The Late Tom Bruce AM
Jannie Brown
Rob & Sal Bruce
Julie Burke
Katie Burke
Geoffrey Bush & Michael Riordan
Pam Caldwell
Helen & Dugald Campbell
John & Jan Campbell
Jessica Canning
Clare Carlson
Jenny & Stephen Charles AO
Chernov Family
Assoc Prof Lyn Clearihan &
    Dr Anthony Palmer
Susan Cohen
Sandy & Yvonne Constantine
Barry & Deborah Conyngham
Karen Cusack
Sue & John Denmead
Mark Duckworth PSM &
    Lauren Mosso
Dr Sally Duguid & Dr David Tingay
Pam Durrant
Bev & Geoff Edwards
Karen & David Elias
Nita Eng
Anne Evans & Graham Evans AO
Marian Evans

Dr Alastair Fearn
Peter Fearnside & Roxane Hislop
Paul & Mary Fildes
Grant Fisher & Helen Bird
Jan & Rob Flew
Rosemary Forbes & Ian Hocking
Bruce Freeman
Gaye & John Gaylard
Howard & Glennys Hocking
Fiona Griffiths & Tony Osmond
Gill Family Foundation
Ian & Wendy Haines
Charles Harkin
M D Harper
Mark & Jennifer Hayes
Luke Heagerty
Lorraine Hendrata
Brett & Kerri Hereward
Dr Alice Hill & Mark Nicholson
Emeritus Prof Andrea Hull AO
Nanette Hunter
Ann & Tony Hyams AM
Peter Jaffe & Judy Gold
Neil Jens
Colin & Helen Masters
Paula McKinnon & Troy Sussman
Ben Johnson & Mark McNamara
Sally & Rod Johnstone
Lesley & Ian Jones
Leah Kaplan & Barry Levy
Irene Kearsey & Michael Ridley
Malcolm Kemp
Daniel Kilby
Michael Kingston
Fiona Kirwan-Hamilton &
    Brett Parkin
Doris & Steve Klein
Marianne & Arthur Klepfisz
Larry Kornhauser & Natalya Gill
Dr Emma Jane Ladakis
Verona Lea

Alison Leslie
Xue Snowe Li
Peter & Judy Loney
Lord Family
Lording Family Foundation
Kerryn Lowe & Raphael Arndt
Ken & Jan Mackinnon
Karin MacNab
Natasha & Laurence Mandie
Chris Maple
Ian & Judi Marshman
Lesley Mason
Penelope McEniry
Heather & Simon McKeon
Garry McLean
Libby McMeekin
Emeritus Prof Peter McPhee AM
Rosemary Meagher &
    The Late Douglas Meagher
Fiona Menzies
Robert & Helena Mestrovic
Ann Miller AM
Ross & Judy Milne-Pott
MK Futures
Barbara & David Mushin
Dr Rosemary Nixon AM
Sarah Nguyen
Nick Nichola & Ingrid Moyle
Michele Nielsen
Dr Paul Nisselle AM & Sue Nisselle
Sally Noonan
David & Lisa Oertle
Dr Jane & Alan Oppenheim
In loving memory of Richard Park
Bruce Parncutt AO
Dr Annamarie Perlesz
Dare & Andrea Power
Peter Philpott & Robert Ratcliffe
D Probert
Philip & Gayle Raftery
Sally Redlich

Victoria Redwood
John & Veronica Rickard
Phillip Riggio
Ken & Gail Roche
Roslyn & Richard Rogers Family
S & S Rogerson
B & J Rollason
Sue Rose
Nick & Rowena Rudge
Jenny Russo
Edwina Sahhar
Margaret Sahhar AM
Sandi Foundation
    dedicated to Alec
Alex & Brady Scanlon Giving Fund
Sally & Tim Scott

FE Scott
Susan Selwyn & Barry Novy
Jacky & Rupert Sherwood
Diane Silk
Dr John Sime
Pauline & Tony Simioni
Jan Simon
Jane Simon & Peter Cox
Tim & Angela Smith
Annette Smorgon
Dr Ross & Helen Stillwell
Rosemary Stipanov
Shannon Super
The Stobart Strauss Foundation
Irene & John Sutton
Rodney & Aviva Taft

Charles Tegner
Frank & Mirium Tisher
John & Anna van Weel
Graham Wademan &
    Michael Bowden
Walter & Gertie Wagner
Kevin & Elizabeth Walsh
Pinky Watson
Kaye & John de Wijn
Ann & Alan Wilkinson
Robert & Diana Wilson
Ralph Wollner &
    The Hon Kirsty Macmillan SC
Mandy & Edward Yencken
Anonymous (27)

EDUCATION GIVING CIRCLE

Acknowledging supporters who are transforming the lives of young Victorians through theatre.

Alan & Mary-Louise
    Archibald Foundation
Joanna Baevski
Judy Bourke
Deborah Conyngham
Geoff Cosgriff
Ann Darby
Linda Herd
Larry Kornhauser OAM &
    Natalya Gill

Greig Gaily & Dr Geraldine Lazarus
Heather & Simon McKeon
The Myer Foundation
Tom & Ruth O'Dea
The Ian Potter Foundation
Christopher Reed
John & Veronica Rickard
Anne & Mark Robertson OAM
Ken & Gail Roche
Roslyn & Richard Rogers Family

Andrew Sisson AO &
    Tracey Sisson
Rob Stewart & Lisa Dowd
The Stirling Family
Ronella Stuart
Ann & Alan Wilkinson
The John & Myriam
    Wylie Foundation
Anonymous (8)

LEGACY CIRCLE

**Acknowledging supporters who have made the visionary gesture of including
a gift to Melbourne Theatre Company in their will.**

John & Lorraine Bates
Mark & Tamara Boldiston
Bernadette Broberg
Adam & Donna Cusack-Muller
Anne Evans & Graham Evans AO
Bruce Freeman
Peter & Betty Game
Edith Gordon

Fiona Griffiths
Linda Herd
Tony Hillery & Warwick Eddington
Jane Kunstler
Irene Kearsey
Robyn & Maurice Lichter
Dr Andrew McAliece &
    Dr Richard Simmie

Libby McMeekin
Peter Philpott & Robert Ratcliffe
Marcus Pettinato
Jillian Smith
Diane Tweeddale
Francis Vergona
Anonymous (14)

Thank you

Melbourne Theatre Company would like to thank the following organisations for their generous support.

Major Partner

Future Directors Initiative Partner

MinterEllison.

Major Marketing Partner

The Monthly
The Saturday Paper
7am

Associate Partners

Challis & Company
Tomorrow's leaders today

Frontier
software
Human Capital Management
& Payroll Software/Services

K&L GATES

THE LANGHAM
MELBOURNE

Supporting Partners

COMMUNE
WINE

Genovese
coffee

invicium

THE
LUXURY
NETWORK®

METROPOLIS
EVENTS

QUEST
SOUTHBANK

southgate

Wilson Parking

Marketing Partners

CINEMA
NOVA

RRR

Southbank Theatre Partners

mgc
THE
MELBOURNE
GIN COMPANY

SCOTCHMANS HILL
BELLARINE PENINSULA
VICTORIA
ESTABLISHED 1982

Business Collective Members

Committee for Melbourne   Leadership Collective Australia   Schuler Shook

Current as of February 2025.

www.ingramcontent.com/pod-product-compliance
Lightning Source LLC
Chambersburg PA
CBHW050026090426
42734CB00021B/3433